PEOPLE OF THE MESA

PEOPLE OF THE MESA

THE ARCHAEOLOGY OF BLACK MESA, ARIZONA

SHIRLEY POWELL

GEORGE J. GUMERMAN

ILLUSTRATIONS BY THOMAS W. GATLIN

SOUTHWEST PARKS AND MONUMENTS ASSOCIATION

TUCSON

SOUTHERN ILLINOIS UNIVERSITY PRESS

CARBONDALE AND EDWARDSVILLE

LIBRARY OF CONGRESS CATALOGING-IN-PUBLICATION DATA

Powell, Shirley, 1948–
  People of the mesa.

  Bibliography: p.
  Includes index.
    1. Indians of North America—Arizona—Black Mesa
(Navajo County and Apache County)—Antiquities.
2. Pueblo Indians—Antiquities.   3. Navajo Indians—
Antiquities.   4. Black Mesa (Navajo County and Apache
County, Ariz.)—Antiquities.   5. Arizona—Antiquities.
I. Gumerman, George J.   II. Title.
E78.A7P69   1987   979.1'35   87-4490
ISBN 0-8093-1400-2

Printed in Japan

Designed by Joyce Kachergis Book Design and Production, Bynum, N.C.

90 89 88 87 4 3 2 1

CONTENTS

ILLUSTRATIONS

FOREWORD

Little did we know when we started that the Black Mesa Archaeological Project would become the largest continuous archaeological project in North America.

Peabody's involvement in archaeological research began in 1966, shortly after we had signed leases to mine coal on Black Mesa in Arizona. Newly passed federal antiquity laws dictated that, before mining could begin in areas where archaeological remains might be endangered, a thorough investigation had to be made and detailed reports filed with governmental agencies.

We had much to learn about these laws and subsequent legislation in the early 1970s, as did the archaeological community, which was just beginning to sort out the complexities of contract archaeology.

Peabody proceeded cautiously. After all, these were new requirements and they represented significant costs and new relationships. The archaeological community had to be involved in our mining plans for the first time, and we needed to develop new procedures to meet the new regulations. But as we experimented, Peabody and the archaeological community gained a mutual understanding and respect. And Peabody's commitment to archaeological investigation was established.

The fieldwork in Arizona spanned seventeen years—every summer from 1967 through 1983. All 64,858 acres in our lease area, which is about

3 percent of the 2.1-million-acre highland known as Black Mesa, were surveyed during that time. Some 2,500 sites were identified, and more than 200 were completely excavated. More than 1 million artifacts, which remain the property of the Navajo and Hopi tribes, were collected and curated for further study by scientists and scholars.

The reports compiled by the Black Mesa archaeologists after each season of fieldwork conform to specific governmental regulations. They are detailed and technical and are valuable resources for the scientific community. But this scientific format leaves a void for the reader who needs interpretation and insight to make past cultures come alive.

Since the early days of the project, we thought that a general-interest book written in lay terms about the Black Mesa Archaeological Project would have merit, and plans for the publication of this book were included in Peabody's budget. We are pleased to be able to share this history of the people who inhabited Black Mesa for thousands of years.

Even though we entered the archaeological milieu rather cautiously twenty years ago, today we look back with a great deal of pride at the discoveries brought about by Peabody's support. We hope it will encourage other cooperative efforts between business and academia and will generate greater enthusiasm for the study and support of archaeology.

ROBERT H. QUENON
President and Chief Executive Officer
Peabody Holding Company, Inc.

ACKNOWLEDGMENTS

More than most, this volume represents the efforts of many people, and we would like to thank some of them here. First and foremost, Peabody Coal Company (Western Division) made this entire undertaking possible by generously supporting the archaeological fieldwork on which this book is based and also by providing the funds for writing and producing it. Gary L. Melvin, head of the Western Division's environmental office, Kenneth R. Moore, president of the Western Division, and Robert H. Quenon, president and Chief Executive Officer of the Peabody Holding Company, were instrumental in encouraging us to make the jump from our usual dry, scientific writings to something that might be more palatable to the many people who are fascinated with archaeology but hesitant to wade through technical reports.

We are anthropologists, trained to study prehistoric remains and to write for people similarly trained. We love our work and find it both exciting and fascinating. Unfortunately, most technical archaeological reports scarcely begin to communicate what it is that draws us to the study of archaeology. And, equally unfortunately, many books about archaeology intended for the general public are incomplete and sensationalized. One of the biggest tasks facing us was to write a book that would be true to our subject matter and would also convey the thrills of discovery, both in the field and in the laboratory. Several people were instrumental in reteaching us to write in

English instead of "scientist-ese." Yvette Duncan and Donna Butler spent many hours with the senior author suggesting and modifying ways to organize and present the text. Yvette was also responsible for editing the manuscript. Her hours of work were crucial to the successful completion of this book. Donna served as "second-string" technical editor, taking over when the job overwhelmed the rest of us. Susan H. Wilson proofread the manuscript before it was sent to press.

The members of the 1984–1985 upper school class at the Carbondale (Illinois) New School were an eager editorial review committee. The senior author spent several mornings talking with them, asking them questions, and being asked questions about how archaeologists find and excavate sites and what they do with the materials they recover. Elizabeth Spees, a member of the class, also read manuscripts of two of the chapters and provided helpful comments.

Other people reviewed parts of the manuscript from a more technical perspective. F. E. Smiley read the Archaic and Basketmaker chapters. His careful consideration of the sections on lithic technology, hunting, and butchering was very informative. William J. Parry also evaluated the discussions of lithic technology, making many well-considered suggestions that were incorporated into the final version. Trish Ruppé researched the seasonal availability of wild plant foods, and Robert Leonard provided valuable information about animal availability. Thomas R. Rocek, Miranda Warburton, and Gerald Vizenor reviewed the chapter on the historic period. Tom and Miranda generously shared their knowledge of Navajo history and prehistory, and conversations with Gerry reminded us that people are people everywhere throughout time.

The illustrations were designed by Robert Dunlavey, and the final versions were drawn by Thomas W. Gatlin. Lynn T. Brittner and Deborah Post, both of the School of American Research, helped track down some of the illustrations used in Chapter 5. Marilyn J. Bender, Jeffrey S. Dean, and Dana B. Oswald also assisted the senior author with identifying potential illustrations. John Richardson, John A. Vercillo, and Karen Schmitt, all of SIUC's Scientific Photography facility, are to be thanked for their assistance and patience.

Marilyn J. Bender, Brenda Wells, and Darren Nix processed the words and corrected (and recorrected) the manuscript. Their expertise and patience are gratefully acknowledged.

PROLOGUE

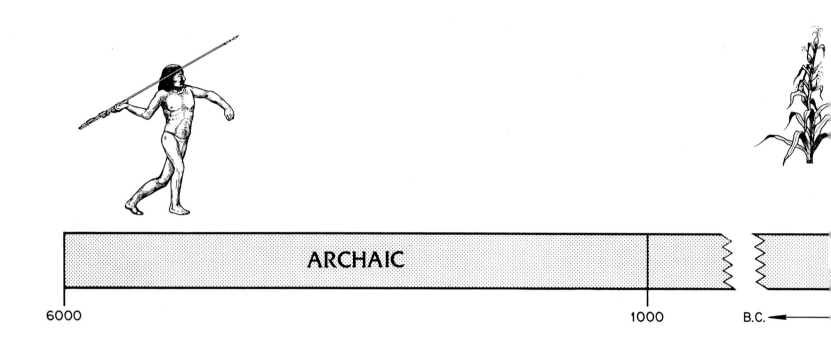

ARCHAIC

6000   1000   B.C. ◄——

Modern archaeology is about more than just artifacts, fine art, or curious objects to grace museum or collectors' shelves. It is a way of understanding how and why humans lived the way they did in the past. Unfortunately, time acts as a filter, and only parts of past cultures survive to be discovered and analyzed by archaeologists. Luckily this filter can be penetrated by archaeological techniques, which analyze material things and how they existed in relationship to one another. And even though there is much more to culture than just material items, the things that archaeologists recover can tell us a great deal about the nonmaterial aspects of culture as well. Archaeologists cannot directly excavate a religion or kinship system; but they can excavate a temple or a rosary, and they can determine the average size of a dwelling and the number of cooking hearths in it. From these types of remains it is possible to reconstruct a belief system and the size and composition of the kin groups that lived together. Some parts of this general sketch of past human behavior are quite clear, some less clear; but archaeologists can infer a way of life and how it changed over time.

To understand how archaeologists reconstruct the past requires more than knowledge of the tools and techniques of excavation (which may range from a camel's-hair brush to a backhoe). Understanding the archaeological history of Black Mesa requires a knowledge of how archaeologists came to be in the area in the first place and how they use modern technology to help them understand a much simpler culture.

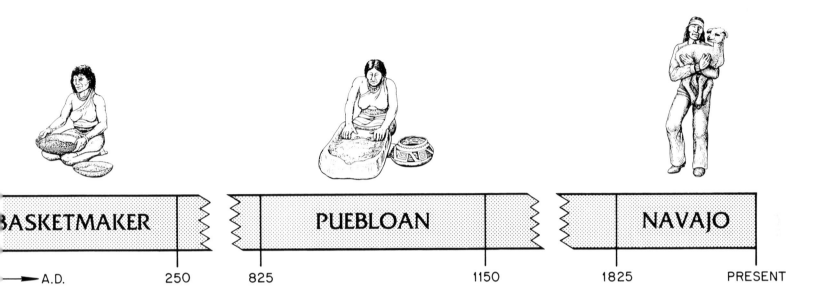

BASKETMAKER   PUEBLOAN   NAVAJO

A.D.   250   825   1150   1825   PRESENT

Figure P-1. The four time periods discussed in this book.

The story that follows is told from several perspectives. Four different occupations of Black Mesa are discussed—each dating to a distinct time period. The Archaic period dates between 6000 and 1000 B.C., before the discovery of agriculture and pottery. The Basketmaker period dates to the beginning of the Christian era; people were growing crops but had not yet invented pottery. The Puebloan period dates between A.D. 825 and 1150, and the people who lived then grew crops and used pottery. The final period, the Navajo occupation, starts about 1825 and continues into the present (Figure P-1).

Our topic is archaeology. We do not address the complex and controversial changes occurring today on Black Mesa. It is beyond the scope of this book to explore the present in any detail. Volumes have already been written about modern energy development and situations of contact between members of diverse cultures by authors trained in psychology, sociology, and political science. We leave the present to them.

Each of these four periods is discussed in its own chapter. Our goal is to show the reader how archaeologists find sites, how the sites are excavated, how the materials recovered from the sites are analyzed, and finally, how all this information is put together to reconstruct how people lived in the past. The descriptions of archaeologists at work are not fictionalized; rather, they are based on the actual field notes taken by real archaeologists working at real sites. This method of reporting is more realistic and less romanticized than most accounts of how archaeologists work. We hope that our more realistic account will communicate to the reader some of the thrills that we have experienced while working on Black Mesa.

The three prehistoric chapters conclude with reconstructions of what life might have been like for the people who lived on Black Mesa during the period covered. The reconstructions are not merely fiction. They are firmly based in the archaeological data, with some elaboration coming from more recent anthropological studies of the Hopi and the Navajo who live on Black Mesa today. As with any reconstruction based on partial evidence, there may be a number of alternative, but equally plausible, interpretations of the same data; and any statements about the thoughts and feelings of preliterate peoples, dead for many centuries, are purely conjecture. Nevertheless, our goal is to provide more than a catalog of prehistoric art. Instead, we have tried to paint a portrait of an extinct way of life.

THE LAND, THE RESOURCES, AND ARCHAEOLOGY

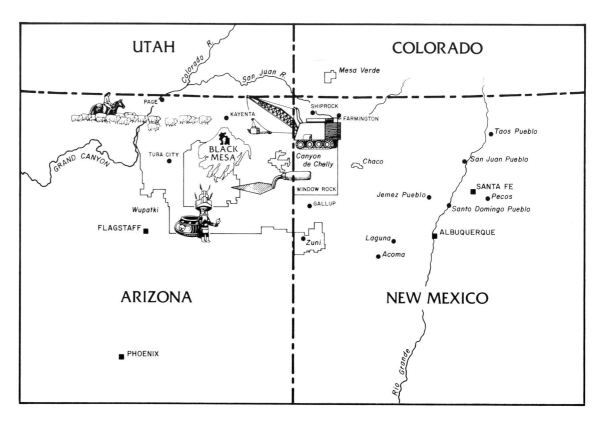

Figure 1-1 (above). From a distance, the heavy vegetation that grows on the scarp and top of Black Mesa gives it a dark appearance. This photograph shows Black Mesa in the foreground, contrasting with the lighter and redder Monument Valley in the distance.

Figure 1-2 (right). Peabody Coal Company is mining coal from lands in northeastern Arizona leased from the Hopi and Navajo Indian tribes. The mining operation has brought together peoples from very different cultures and backgrounds: the Hopis, descendants of the prehistoric Anasazi inhabitants of Black Mesa; the Navajos, who moved into the American Southwest from the north at about the same time as the Spanish conquistadors moved in from the south; and the Euroamericans, including Peabody Coal Company employees and archaeologists.

Black Mesa is a huge land mass in northeastern Arizona, some seventy-five miles in diameter. Its name comes from its dark appearance, which is caused by the dense stands of pinyon and juniper trees that cover its slopes. The mesa contrasts starkly with the surrounding barren sandstone landscape; even from great distances, Black Mesa stands dark and massive as one of the most dominant features of the southwestern geography (Figure 1-1).

This book is about the interaction of four cultures—the Anasazi, the Hopi, the Navajo, and Euroamericans—all of whom have come together on northern Black Mesa (Figure 1-2). The book's central concern is archaeology, but not in the usual sense of long dead cultures, forgotten languages, and searches for spectacular or ancient keys to the past. Rather, this is the story of the interpretation of an old way of life from the remains of two living, vibrant cultures, the Hopi and the Navajo (Figures 1-3, 1-4). It is also the story of how the world's largest coal company, Peabody Coal, came to be involved in archaeological research in its mining **lease area*** in Arizona. The Hopi, the Navajo, the coal company, and the archaeologists all helped to put together a picture of over two thousand years of changing prehistory and history in Arizona.

* Words in boldface are listed in the glossary.

Figure 1-3 (left). The Hopis live in apartment-house-type pueblos located on fingerlike extensions of southern Black Mesa. Although the Hopis enjoy access to modern technological innovations like electricity, motorized vehicles, and canned foods, their villages are still much like the pueblos first encountered by the Spaniards in 1520.

Figure 1-4 (right). The Navajos live in camps, or compounds, of several related families. Each family occupies its own hogan and shares access to the large sheep and horse corrals used to pen the livestock.

Figure 1-5. Northern Black Mesa rises an imposing two thousand feet above the adjacent Monument Valley; along its southern scarp the mesa is eroded and "fingers" into the Hopi Mesas, some five hundred feet above the surrounding landscape.

THE LAND: PRESENT AND PAST

Black Mesa is sometimes described as a giant hand, palm up and slightly cupped, with the fingers tilting down and pointing to the southwest. The fingers are the extensions of Black Mesa known as the Hopi Mesas, for that is where the still occupied Hopi villages are. The heel of the hand on the northeast is the highest point of this two-million-acre uplift, rising some two thousand feet, overlooking the stark and dramatic Monument Valley (Figure 1-5). More immediately to the north are Long House and Klethla valleys, with the famous picturesque cliff dwellings of Betatakin, Kiet Siel, and Inscription House only fifteen miles north of the mesa (Figure 1-6). Elevation drops markedly from the north of the mesa to the south, and that affects the kinds and amounts of vegetation as well as the availability of water. Washes, trending in a southwestern direction, have cut deeply into the top of the mesa. They flow only after heavy rains and snowmelt. The more rugged country is in the north, and rolling hills dominate the landscape to the south.

Pinyon and juniper are dense at the higher elevations in the north, especially on the slopes and ridges, but there are many open areas covered with grasses and, in the deeper soil, sagebrush (Figure 1-7). In the narrow can-

Figure 1-6 (above). Black Mesa is bordered on the north by mesas and valleys carved into the red Navajo Sandstone. In one of these valleys, the Tsegi Canyon system, there are some spectacular cliff houses.

Figure 1-7 (left). The lease area is characterized by rolling hills and rugged angular rock outcrops, covered with pinyon and juniper trees. The land is divided by southwesterly trending washes whose floodplains are vegetated with sage and grasses.

Figure 1-8. Isolated stands of ponderosa pine, scrub oak, and Douglas fir are found in the deeply incised canyons just north of the lease area. An erosion-resistant sandstone caps the coal-bearing deposits here, creating sheer-walled canyons.

yons at the heads of washes are isolated stands of Douglas fir, ponderosa pine, and scrub oak (Figure 1-8). Springs are found in the upper reaches of the canyons, but more often in the south near the Hopi villages (Figures 1-9, 1-10). Water, however, is generally in short supply; rainfall is scarce, and much of it falls as very localized summer thundershowers. Only then do the washes carry water, but the stream flow is so rapid that erosion occurs and little water is absorbed into the ground. All in all, it is a visually dramatic environment, one in which by all appearances it would be difficult to make a living, especially for farmers.

The archaeologists' task is to determine how the prehistoric peoples existed in such a barren and changeable landscape. To do so it is necessary to determine what kind of environment they had to confront and, if necessary, manipulate. Preindustrial peoples were closely related to their environment. They did not, of course, have many of the technological advantages, such as irrigation pumps, that shield us from the whims of nature. They also did not have the national or even global social and economic networks that exist today, and so were more dependent on local environmental conditions and variations. Relief efforts for drought-stricken areas could not be mounted from thousands of miles away as they can be today. Prehistoric peoples did, however, have a remarkably efficient means of adapting to their unpredictable environment, as we shall see.

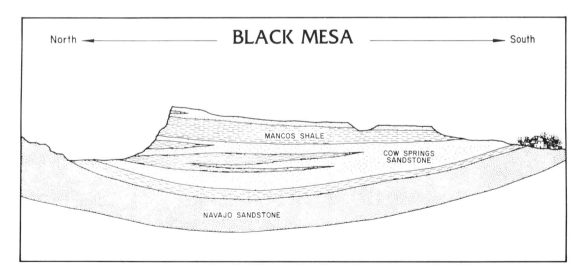

Figure 1-9 (above). Marsh Pass, viewed from the southwest. The pink Navajo Sandstone rise on the left is Skeleton Mesa, and the gray-green uplift on the right is Black Mesa.

Figure 1-10 (left). Black Mesa is composed of several smaller plateaus, which in turn are made up of coal-bearing sandstone and shale capped by erosion-resistant sandstone. The Navajo Sandstone forms the surface sediments north of Black Mesa. It dips beneath the mesa, where, because it is less permeable than the overlying sediments, it forms a pool of underground water (or aquifer). The Navajo Sandstone and the aquifer re-emerge along the southern scarp of the mesa, forming a number of dependable springs.

Figure 1-11. When the water table was high and rainfall abundant, slowly moving floodwaters deposited silt, building up the land surface. Hydrologic and geomorphologic studies have documented the existence of natural dams formed by sediments deposited at the confluences of major washes. Water ponded behind these dams, forming small pockets of water-dependent flora and fauna in an otherwise barren environment.

Our reconstruction of the past environment of Black Mesa was accomplished by using the results of tree-ring, geological, and plant pollen studies. It is possible to analyze the past environment by examining tree rings, because tree-ring width is highly correlated with climate, especially precipitation, in the Southwest. A wide annual growth ring indicates favorable, wetter conditions; the assumption is that if it was a good year for tree growth, it was probably also a good year for domesticated crops.

Close examination of the recent geology provides evidence for the reconstruction of past rainfall and groundwater patterns. Hydrological conditions leave their evidence on sands, gravels, and soils. When surface water was abundant, floods were frequent, and slowly moving streams deposited silt and sand, building up the land's surface. When the climate was dry, the water table fell; at such times, infrequent but torrential seasonal rains caused erosion and **arroyo** cutting. Arroyo, or gully, cutting also occurred during the transition between wet and dry periods (Figure 1-11).

Past vegetation patterns are reconstructed through pollen analysis, or **palynology** (Box 1-1). Pollen grains of individual plants preserve well and are highly distinctive; since individual species may therefore be identified (Figure 1-12), it is possible to get an idea of the composition of the plant cover and how it might have changed through time.

The best example of how interdisciplinary research has worked to con-

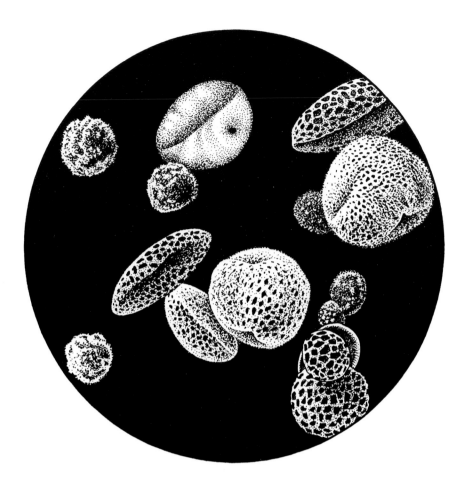

Figure 1-12. Pollen grains are very distinctive and can be used to identify the species of plant that produced them.

struct an image of past environmental and cultural worlds comes from the interior of the mesa, considerably south of the coal lease area. In 1976, archaeologists and geologists from the project visited some reported ruins with high standing walls. The sites proved to date to A.D. 1250, after the Anasazi abandoned what is now the coal lease area. More important, however, was the discovery that there were buried juniper trees exposed in the sides of the arroyo that dissected the canyon. These trees were killed by sand and soil that had washed rapidly into the valley. Even though they were buried, they remained standing, often with small twigs and needles still attached to the branches (Figure 1-13). Once the buried trees were discovered in the arroyo walls, others were found whose topmost branches poked above the surface of the ground. Near the sides of the low canyon were young living junipers that were in the process of being buried (Figure 1-14).

In this small valley, only a quarter-mile wide and less than a mile long, the potential existed for understanding and dating the cycles of environmental change. The dead juniper trees were killed by rapid deposition of water-transported sediments. Several such depositional cycles, which occurred during periods of heavier-than-average rainfall, were recorded by the dead but still standing trees. Pollen samples were taken from contexts **associated** with the trees to aid in the reconstruction of vegetation pat-

Box 1-1. Plant pollen is frequently transported from plants to archaeological sites by wind, animals, or people who harvest the plants. Some pollen then settles into the soil, where it may fossilize—turn to stone. This pollen can be extracted from the soil and identified by trained scientists known as palynologists, whose findings help the archaeologist to ascertain what plants were growing near the site when it was occupied and what plants were used by Native Americans. Both kinds of information are helpful both for reconstructing the environment and for figuring out how it was exploited by the occupants.

Figure 1-13. The junipers that gave their name to Dead Juniper Wash were found eroding out of the wash that cut through the middle of the canyon. Other dead and dying trees were found near the sides of the canyon.

terns. And the archaeological remains and tree-ring samples were used to date the tree-killing episodes and the intervening dry periods.

The various techniques were used in combination to reconstruct a general picture of the past environment. The relatively accurate dates, from archaeological remains and tree rings associated with the different environmental conditions, make it possible to determine when changes occurred in the vegetation, precipitation, and hydrology—environmental factors that are critical to human existence.

CULTURAL AND ENVIRONMENTAL INTERACTIONS

Once environmental conditions have been reconstructed, archaeologists study human responses to changes in those conditions. So the next step is to compare the natural record with the archaeological one. A comparison of cultural conditions (recorded by archaeological remains) and natural conditions at different times then gives clues to how the environment affected people. The danger is in assuming that there is a one-to-one correlation between environmental change and cultural change and that all cultural change is a result of adaptation to changes in the natural world.

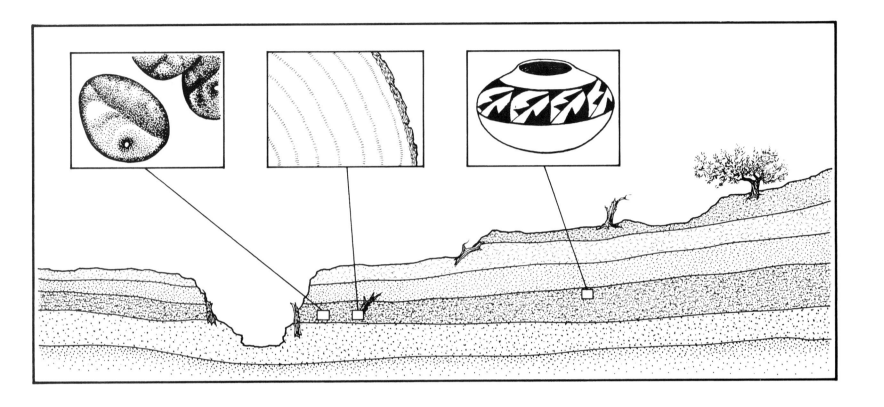

Even a cursory examination of our own culture clearly shows that humans too form part of the environment. New Yorkers are obviously stressed by other New Yorkers during a rush-hour subway ride, and anyone who has read about acid rain and industrial pollution cannot help being concerned with the impact humans have on their physical environment. Archaeologists and their colleagues in the natural sciences, therefore, must be attuned to the nuances and complexities of both culture and nature and not see one as responding mechanically to changes in the other. Furthermore, no culture, not even our own, can anticipate, read, and interpret the environment correctly at all times; therefore, incorrect decisions are made about how to respond to the natural world. As the archaeological record shows, a series of wrong decisions about how to respond to the natural world has often been fatal to the survival of the culture.

So what did all this fieldwork and theorizing tell us about the past environment on Black Mesa? Essentially, it was not much different from today. There was more ground cover, mostly grasses, and the soil was somewhat thicker on the ridges and slopes. The denuding of the area occurred in historic times—probably, in part, the result of overgrazing by large herds of sheep, goats, and cattle, and of a dry period in the environmental cycle. A marginal environment such as Black Mesa, however, could not tolerate much in the way of temperature or rainfall variation without severe con-

Figure 1-14. The dead juniper trees exposed by the wash and along the sides of the canyon were killed by the same process, but at different times. Archaeological remains and tree-ring samples were used to date the death of the trees, and pollen samples were collected and used to reconstruct the vegetation growing in the canyon at the times the trees were killed and between these times.

sequences for the vegetation, and the domesticated crops of the Anasazi would have been especially vulnerable. Small shifts in the pattern of when rainfall occurred, or an inch or two difference in annual precipitation, could mean disaster for this agricultural population.

COAL MINING ON BLACK MESA

Peabody officials focused their attention on Black Mesa in the early 1960s. At that time, only oil, gas, and water power were being used to generate electricity in the Southwest, but projected consumer demands indicated that new sources of energy would be needed in the near future. Low-sulfur, high-quality coal was known to be plentiful in the Four Corners region, the area where Utah, Colorado, Arizona, and New Mexico come together. Coal **outcrops** and smoldering areas where underground coal had ignited, perhaps as long as a century ago, were visible in many places. It was known that there was coal on northern Black Mesa, for that area had been the scene of a small-scale attempt at commercial coal mining in the 1940s. Coal was shipped by wagon and truck from Black Mesa to the

school at Tuba City, some sixty miles to the west. But the high cost of transportation had made a larger-scale effort uneconomical.

With exploration permits from the Navajo and Hopi tribes and the U.S. Geological Survey, Peabody drilled about ten thousand test holes in the early 1960s. They determined that high-quality underground coal existed in seams from four to thirty feet thick, close enough for surface mining. By 1966, mining leases were signed with the two tribes, and contracts were formalized with utility companies to supply coal to the Mohave Generating Plant in southern Nevada and to the Navajo Generating Plant at Lake Powell.

The transportation problem was solved in two ways. The crushed coal was mixed with water from deep wells and pumped through an underground pipeline 275 miles from Black Mesa to the Nevada power plant, and a railroad was built to carry coal from the base of Black Mesa ninety miles north to Lake Powell (Figure 1-15). But this is only the most recent chapter in the story of coal mining in Black Mesa.

Long before there was ever a thought about the use of coal for electricity, before electricity was even generated, even before the Spanish entered the Southwest, there was coal mining on Black Mesa. Coal seams outcrop at several places on the mesa and along the southern rim, where the Hopi

Figure 1-15. The power plants that burn the Black Mesa coal are located at Lake Powell (90 miles from the mines) and at Bullhead City, Nevada (275 miles from the mines). The crushed coal is transported to the Navajo Generating Plant at Lake Powell via the Black Mesa–Lake Powell Railroad, which was built solely to transport the coal. Coal destined for the Nevada power plant is crushed, mixed with water, and pumped through a pipeline from Black Mesa to Bullhead City.

Figure 1-16.(above and right). Prehistoric Hopis used some coal for firing a distinctive and beautiful type of pottery made during the 1400s and 1500s. The high temperatures generated by the coal firing helped produce the characteristic yellow background color of these ceramics. Earlier Black Mesa peoples also used coal to fire some of their pottery. Pottery dated to A.D. 825 found in the lease area also has the characteristic yellow background caused by coal firing. Hopi pottery from the collections of the Museum of North Arizona, Flagstaff.

villages exist today. Prehistoric Native Americans mined this coal with wood, stone, and antler tools; they followed the outcrops inward, removing sandstone overburden to expose the coal. Geologists estimate that more than 27,000 tons of coal were mined adjacent to the villages of Awatovi alone, enough to supply the village with almost half a ton of coal per day during the entire three hundred years that it was occupied.

Archaeologists excavating in the large villages occupied by the ancestors of the Hopi have found great quantities of burned coal ash. Some of the ash is from hearths inside dwelling units, some is found in village trash heaps, and some is found right next to the tailings from the prehistoric strip mines. The coal ash found in homes and in the trash is probably the remains of heating and cooking fuel. The ashpiles found adjacent to the mines themselves were also associated with numerous pottery **sherds** and, in one case, with a cache of whole pots. This coal was probably used to **fire** pottery; and because the clay and coal deposits have been found in close proximity, researchers have postulated that the clay was mined, formed into vessels, and fired all in one place (Figure 1-16; Box 1-2).

Archaeologists cease to find evidence of the use of coal for cooking, heating, and pottery manufacture at about A.D. 1700. This date coincides with

the widespread movement of Spaniards and their domesticated herd animals into the area. Sheep and goats, besides being a source of meat, fiber, and hides, are a source of fuel. The Hopi currently use sheep dung for firing pottery, and archaeologists conjecture that dung replaced coal as a fuel source in about 1700.

It is interesting that coal mining has such a long history on Black Mesa, because the modern Peabody mines are the reasons for one of the longest-running and largest archaeological projects in North America. To Peabody's surprise, when the coal company had completed the lease negotiations, they were informed that under federal and tribal laws they were required to investigate any archaeological remains that might be endangered by their operations. Since Peabody had never mined on federally controlled tribal lands, they were unaware of these requirements; they knew nothing about how archaeologists work or even how to contact them.

Eventually, Peabody's engineers negotiated with archaeologists from the now defunct Prescott College, and fieldwork commenced in 1967. The project was later transferred to Southern Illinois University. Each year, arrangements were made for the archaeologists to work in advance of the mining operations so that representative information about past lifeways

Box 1-2. Some of the coal was used to fire the beautiful yellow pottery that was produced in late prehistoric times, just before the arrival of the Spanish. The characteristic yellow background, produced in part by the high firing temperature that coal provides, is found in about 1 percent of the pottery on northern Black Mesa from the time when pottery was first made there, about A.D. 825. Apparently, there were always a few vessels that were coal-fired, but we do not know whether coal firing was chosen because of the yellowish background it produced or because it resulted in a harder vessel with a more brittle wall.

could be excavated prior to mining activities. At this date, 2,500 prehistoric and historic sites have been recorded and 200 of them excavated, at a cost to the coal and power companies of approximately six million dollars.

What have we learned with this six million dollars? And what were the methods used to gain this information? Archaeologists must work with scientists from many fields, from climatology and geology to sociology, in order to gather all the information necessary to reconstruct ancient cultures. And once past lifeways are reconstructed, the question becomes how and why did those cultures change? In a sense, archaeology is the study of failed attempts at coping with physical environments and other peoples, since archaeological sites have been abandoned and the people who created them have either moved on or died out. Archaeologists want to know why. The rest of this book sketches what the archaeologists learned about how the inhabitants of northern Black Mesa adapted to its formidable landscape and in what ways they failed.

ARCHAIC

CHAPTER 2

Figure 2-1 (left). Before excavation, site D:11:3063 consisted of a few sandstone slabs set on end into the sandy soil and several pieces of chipped stone that were flaked off during the production of stone tools.

Figure 2-2 (right). Archaeological surveyors discover sites by walking over the land and systematically looking for signs of previous occupations, such as potsherds or chipped stone. Spaced ten to twenty feet apart, the surveyors mark the edge of each transect with paper markers so they know exactly where they have been and where they will go next.

SURVEY: JUNE 16, 1980

The archaeologist looked up from her topographic map and scanned the surrounding landscape of rolling, sage-covered hills. Her five-person crew had stopped when one crew member noticed some bright red pieces of **chipped stone.** The rest of the crew was looking for more signs of an archaeological site while the crew chief was trying to find their exact location on the map (Figure 2-1).

The survey crew, which was one of five working in the Peabody Coal Company lease, had been given the job of locating all the sites in a seven-square-mile area. Since late May they had been systematically walking in **transects** the entire area shown on the map (Figure 2-2). On this particular day they were **surveying** just south of Yucca Flat Wash and had already located, mapped, and collected artifacts from four sites. This was their fifth, and the lack of pottery on its surface promised a very old site.

Close examination of the area revealed about fifteen variously colored pieces of chipped stone and three sandstone slabs set on end in the sandy topsoil. The crew set a **datum** stake for a reference point, drew a map showing the locations of the chipped stone and the stone slabs, and marked the location of the site (now designated site D:11:3063 [SIUC]; Box 2-1) on their **base map** (Figure 2-3). On the form they filled out, they noted the

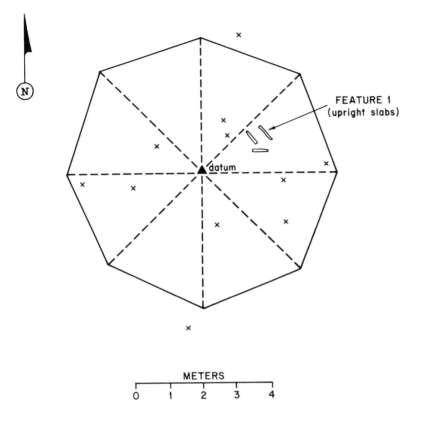

FEATURE 1
(upright slabs)

datum

METERS

0   1   2   3   4

×   Lithic artifacts (not all shown)

Figure 2-3. Site boundaries are identified by measuring sudden changes in the kinds and numbers of artifacts on the site's surface. The distance between the datum and these discontinuities is measured at eight points, forming an irregular eight-sided boundary.

many different kinds of chipped stone and suggested that the upright slabs were the remains of a hearth. Most important, however, was the total absence of pottery, which suggested that the site had been abandoned before pottery was introduced into the Southwest.

EXCAVATION: JUNE 1982

The excavators had been working at site D:11:3063 for three weeks and had uncovered a large area. Their first task had been to relocate the datum stake left behind by the surveyors two years earlier. Finding the foot-high wooden stake among the many knee-high sage plants was time-consuming, but while they searched for it, they looked over the entire area of the site and familiarized themselves with the location of artifacts.

After they found the stake, the excavators set up a transit and mapped the location of a new off-site datum that would be out of the way of the excavations. The new datum was the single point from which they would map and measure the depth of all materials taken from the site (Figure 2-4). Then they divided the site into 2 × 2–meter squares and cleared the vegetation so that they could see the ground better. The locations of all the surface artifacts were plotted on the map before they were collected. They

Box 2-1. Sites are assigned numbers using the Arizona Quadrangle System. The entire state of Arizona is divided into thirty-two quadrangles, each 1 degree of longitude by 1 degree latitude. The quadrangles are labeled with letters of the alphabet, from *A* to *Z* and *AA* to *FF.* The quadrangles are subdivided into sixteen sectors, each identified with a number between one and sixteen. The designation, site D:11:3063 (SIUC), means that the site is situated in sector 11 of the D quadrangle. The final number in the site designation is assigned by the institution that found the site—in this case, Southern Illinois University at Carbondale. Often such numbers are assigned in a simple 1-2-3 sequence, but the SIUC archaeologists use a system that encodes information about the site type (prehistoric) and the site size (smaller than 160 square meters).

Since archaeologists from different institutions maintain their own numbering systems, a site surveyed by more than one institution may have two or more different numbers. All sites discussed in this book were discovered by SIUC archaeologists, so "(SIUC)" has been omitted from the site number.

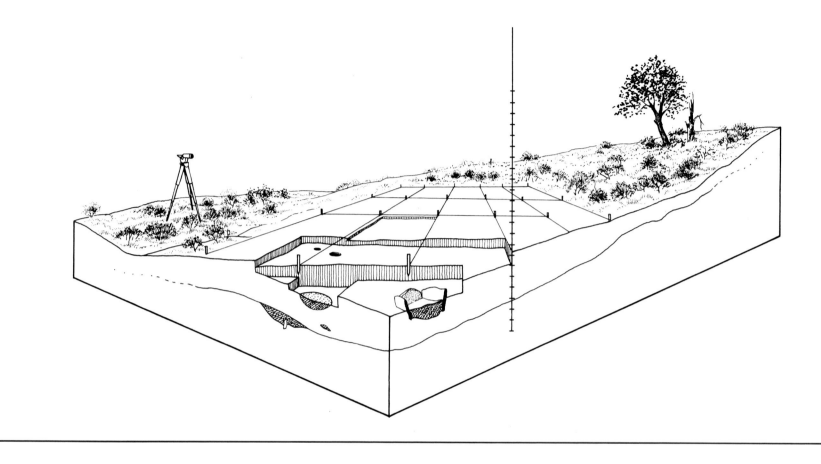

Figure 2-4. All artifacts, features, and structures are measured in three-dimensional space and are identified by coordinates tied in with an off-site datum.

were then collected and placed in bags that were carefully labeled to show the laboratory analysts exactly from which 2 × 2−meter unit the enclosed artifacts came.

While some of the archaeologists were collecting the surface artifacts, others mapped the contours and all stones and differences in soil color on the surface of the site. Site D:11:3063 was located on a low ridge that gently sloped to a dry wash; thus any large sandstone slabs or low spots in the surface had probably been caused by **structures** built, used, and abandoned by the prehistoric inhabitants. Any dark-stained soil might mark the location of charcoal and ash left in a hearth.

All this information was plotted on the field map to help determine what to excavate. What the archaeologists learned from the surface alone was enough to tell them that no **pithouses** or masonry structures were present but that several hearths had been built and used. The lack of pottery indicated that the site had been occupied at least 1,500 years ago, and the types of chipped stone artifacts suggested that the inhabitants were there long enough to make or resharpen a **projectile point.**

After completing the surface collection and mapping of site D:11:3063, the archaeologists devised an excavation plan (Box 2-2). They decided to excavate the areas around the three sandstone slabs and the charcoal/ash staining because they were the only definite remains of prehistoric human

Figure 2-5. All soil excavated from the site is sieved through quarter-inch mesh. All materials too large to fall through the screen are examined by archaeologists, and all artifacts and questionable materials are saved and sent to the laboratory.

activity; figuring out where to dig on the rest of the site was more difficult. Because there wasn't time to excavate the entire site, the archaeologists had to choose a sample. The boundaries of the site had been redefined to include 260 square meters, or sixty-five 2 × 2−meter units. Twelve 2 × 2−meter units (18.5 percent of the area) positioned throughout the entire site area were selected. But because excavations were expanded as interesting **features** or artifacts were uncovered, thirty-five 2 × 2−meter units were eventually excavated.

Although the archaeologists worked within 2 × 2−meter units, all artifacts and other samples taken from the site were located and mapped within 1 × 1−meter units. A 1 × 1 was too small to dig in, and a 2 × 2 was too large for pinpointing the location of artifacts. Excavating the four 1 × 1−meter units within the 2 × 2−meter unit provided enough room to work and the mapping precision necessary for analysis.

As the soil was removed, it was screened through quarter-inch mesh (Figure 2-5) to ensure that all materials of any significant size would be recovered. Some of the screened materials were clearly artifacts; others were not and were discarded and carted off the site with the dirt from the excavations. Some other materials could not definitely be identified as artifacts in the field. All the artifacts and questionable items were put in labeled bags and trucked to the field laboratory at the end of each day. There

Box 2-2. Archaeologists face a dilemma because they will find things only where they look. Thus, if they look only where they know certain things lie buried, those are the things they will find and new discoveries may never be made. To avoid this problem, archaeologists on Black Mesa have figured out a way to choose portions of less promising areas for excavation and to extend that information to the entire site. This does not mean that additional areas of the site cannot be excavated if something exceptional is found; it does mean that archaeologists can excavate a portion of a site and then say with a specified degree of certainty whether other remains might be found.

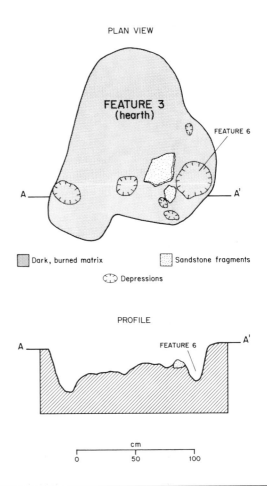

PLAN VIEW

FEATURE 3
(hearth)

FEATURE 6

A ——— A'

Dark, burned matrix   Sandstone fragments

Depressions

PROFILE

A   FEATURE 6   A'

cm
0   50   100

Figure 2-6 (left). Soil samples are taken from most levels of most excavation units. One type of sample is sent to the field laboratory for flotation. There it is dumped into a large barrel of water. The soil is carefully sieved through a fine-mesh screen so that only the very small materials caught in the screen and the lighter-than-water materials (the light fraction) that float to the water's surface remain. The light fraction is skimmed from the surface, dried, and examined under a microscope. It might include parts of insects, modern plants, and ancient plant material that had burned and carbonized. The carbonized seeds and charcoal are direct evidence of what Native Americans ate and how they prepared their food.

The heavier-than-water materials (the heavy fraction) include materials so small that they fall through the quarter-inch mesh when the soil is screened in the field. Most commonly recovered are very small animal bones and some of the waste flakes from chipped stone tool production, although occasionally tiny beads are found.

Figure 2-7 (right). Features are carefully mapped in plan and profile, and much information is recorded about them by the field archaeologists. The archaeologists use this information to determine how the feature was built and what it was used for.

they were analyzed, and the questionable items were carefully examined to determine whether they were natural (and could be discarded) or cultural (and deserved further analysis).

As the excavations at site D:11:3063 proceeded, many artifacts, **flotation samples** (Figure 2-6), and **pollen samples** were collected, carefully numbered and labeled, and sent to the laboratory for more detailed examination. The excavations also uncovered the remains of building activities that were too small to have been houses or structures. These twelve remains, called features by the archaeologists, included one hearth and one roasting pit. However, ten of the features were simply circular or rectangular pits. They could be distinguished because they were filled with soil of a different color and texture than the surrounding soil. Some of the features contained chipped stone artifacts or charcoal, but most were filled only with dark brown or yellowish red soil.

The excavators filled out special forms and drew a map and **profile** for each feature (Figure 2-7). The forms asked for information about size, shape, and depth; the materials inside the feature (its **fill**); artifacts and other samples taken from the feature; and structures or artifacts found nearby that might have been used at the same time as the feature (its **context**).

Since site D:11:3063 had no ceramic artifacts, it was especially important for the archaeologists to collect materials that would help date it. The

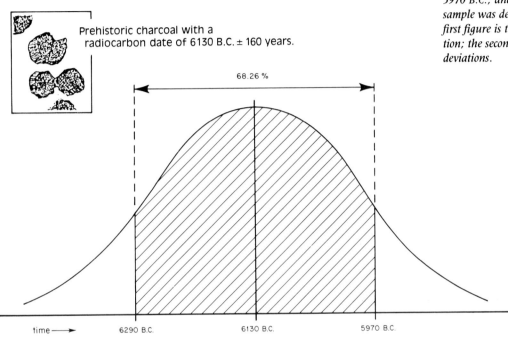

Prehistoric charcoal with a
radiocarbon date of 6130 B.C. ± 160 years.

68.26 %

time ⟶   6290 B.C.   6130 B.C.   5970 B.C.

Figure 2-8. The plus-or-minus figure, or standard deviation, associated with a radiocarbon date allows the archaeologists to determine that the actual site date falls within a specified interval. For the date 6130 B.C. ± 160, we can be 68 percent certain that the actual date the sample was deposited is between 6290 and 5970 B.C., and we can be 95 percent certain that the sample was deposited between 6450 and 5810 B.C. The first figure is the date plus or minus one standard deviation; the second is the date plus or minus two standard deviations.

absence of pottery suggested that the site was old but by itself was not conclusive proof. There was always the possibility that ceramic-period occupants of Black Mesa had made the site but had not left any broken pottery there. To eliminate this possibility the archaeologists needed material, preferably from several different contexts, that would provide an **absolute date**, a date that could be interpreted in real calendar years. The charcoal from the hearth and roasting pit offered the best possibilities for absolute dating (Box 2-3).

The archaeologists collected several charcoal samples from the features at site D:11:3063. Two were sent to a laboratory that specializes in dating carbon samples. The analysis of the materials yielded dates to support the archaeologists' interpretation that the site was very old: 5860 B.C. ± 500 and 6130 B.C. ± 160 (Figure 2-8). These dates were several thousand years older than any others from Black Mesa carbon samples. (At the conclusion of fieldwork in 1983, only one other site that old had been found.)

Little remained at site D:11:3063 when the fieldwork was finished. The artifacts had been sifted from the soil, soil had been collected for flotation and pollen analyses, charcoal had been removed from the features, and the features themselves had been taken apart to determine how they had been constructed. Ironically, in order to preserve information about the site, the site itself had been destroyed. However, all the work had been done in such

Box 2-3. All living things absorb radioactive carbon (carbon 14, or C-14) from the atmosphere. When they die, no new C-14 is absorbed and the C-14 absorbed during life changes back to a stable form: carbon 12, or C-12. The transformation from C-14 to C-12 takes place at a predictable rate, so archaeologists can determine how long something has been dead by determining how much of its C-14 has been converted into C-12. Generally, about one cup of charcoal is necessary for dating with this technique. Techniques have recently been developed that will date much smaller amounts of organic material, but they are very expensive.

Figure 2-9 (left). All artifacts and samples taken from the site are transported to the field laboratory and inventoried every day.

Figure 2-10 (right). Artifacts are washed so that their important attributes can be more easily identified.

a controlled and systematic manner that the archaeologists could have reconstructed the site if necessary. This, in a way, was what the analysts were doing in the field laboratory.

ANALYSIS: JUNE AND JULY 1982

At the end of each day of fieldwork, the excavators brought the artifacts and samples to the field laboratory. They had already bagged, labeled, and inventoried the materials, and the laboratory assistants' first task was to verify that everything taken from the site actually made it into the laboratory (Figure 2-9).

Once inventoried, the materials were subdivided by category and taken to the proper analysts. Flotation samples went to the **ethnobotanical** lab; pollen and C-14 samples were stored temporarily; and the stone artifacts went to the specialists in stone tools. By starting analysis while excavations were ongoing, the archaeologists ensured that no materials were inadvertently lost while awaiting transfer to the main laboratory at Southern Illinois University and that the analytical results would be available to help guide and interpret the excavations.

The **soil samples** collected for flotation underwent water separation

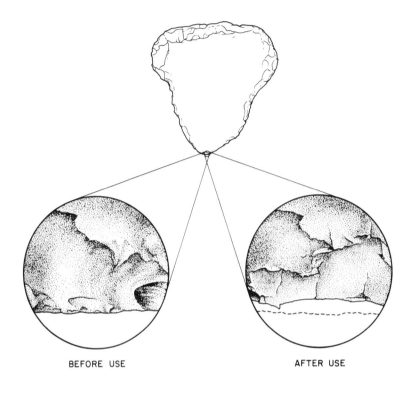

BEFORE USE   AFTER USE

within a day or so after they were sent to the laboratory. Botanists examined the light fraction and identified the **carbonized** materials. Artifacts found in the heavy fraction were given to the appropriate analyst.

The chipped stone, or **lithic,** artifacts were carefully washed before they were analyzed (Figure 2-10). Washing removed dirt and other debris that might obscure what the analysts were looking for. When the artifacts were dry, the laboratory workers used pen and ink to label each one with its site and bag number. Each bag of artifacts had been given a number in the field that corresponded to a number on the inventory sheets. By labeling the artifact with the site and bag numbers, the artifact's exact location could be determined by checking the inventory sheet, even if the artifact was taken out of the bag. Without a record of context, the artifacts would be of little value in figuring out how the site had been used.

Some 197 pieces of chipped stone were found on the site. Most (176) were waste **flakes** from tool production or refurbishing, and twenty-nine of these could be identified as coming from **biface** production (Figures 2-11, 2-12).

The sixteen tools found at site D:11:3063 included eight flakes that had been used for cutting or scraping, but had not been otherwise shaped. Two projectile points, two drills, two bifaces, and one scraper were identified, as was one **core** (the piece of stone from which the flakes or blades were

Figure 2-11 (left). The type of debris, or "debitage," remaining from chipped stone tool production tells the archaeologist a great deal about how the tool was made. An "expedient" tool is a flake that has been knocked off the core and used with no further modification. The debris from a flake tool is different from that of a biface, a tool carefully shaped by removing small flakes from both edges. Biface debitage includes the larger flakes resulting from roughing out the tool shape as well as the thinning flakes from the final production stages.

Figure 2-12 (right). Microscopic examination of the utilized edge of a chipped stone tool can tell archaeologists about the tool's function. Cutting causes a different kind of edge damage from scraping, and using the tool on different materials also causes distinctive kinds of damage. Additionally, residues such as the opalescent material in grasses may build up on the used edge of a tool. Each of these traces provides the archaeologist with important information on how a tool was used.

struck) (Box 2-4). Five pieces of unworked stone were also found. These were distinctive because they were types of stone that do not occur naturally in the area around the site and therefore must have been brought in by the inhabitants.

Twenty-four different types of stone were found on the site. Several of these appear naturally on Black Mesa and were presumably collected by the inhabitants in the course of their wanderings on the mesa. However, many are found only off the mesa—some from as far as 150 miles away. Several kinds of chipped stone artifacts were made from one type of raw material. Waste flakes, **biface thinning flakes** and very small chips, two **utilized flakes,** one biface, and two projectile points were all made from obsidian. Since this was a full range of the type of debris, or **reduction sequence,** that would result from tool production, it seemed likely that projectile points had been actually made at the site.

Analysis of the **organic** materials that were excavated might shed some light on how the stone tools had been used. No bones were found, but the light fraction from the flotation samples was dried and examined through a microscope (Figure 2-13). Modern organic debris, such as juniper and pinyon needles and insect parts, was sorted out; and the remaining material, the charred plant parts, was identified by comparing it to a type collection. The type collection included modern leaves, stems, and seeds that had been

Figure 2-13. An ethnobotanist examines the light fraction from a flotation sample.

intentionally charred by the botanists. Because burning often distorts characteristic features of the plants, it was important that the botanists have similarly burned materials for comparison. For instance, a burned corn kernel might not look like an unburned one, but it could be identified by comparing it with another burned kernel.

The results of the flotation analysis were disappointing but not unusual. Rabbitbrush charcoal came from Feature 11, one of the slab-lined hearths, and from Feature 1, a hemispherical pit. Feature 1 also had pinyon charcoal in its fill, as did Feature 5, another hemispherical pit. Charcoal from an unidentifiable conifer came from Feature 3, the large roasting pit. This charcoal looked like conifer wood, but the analyst could not determine exactly what kind of evergreen tree or shrub produced it (probably pinyon or pine).

The absence of other types of charred plant remains does not mean that other plants were not used on site D:11:3063. The archaeologists figured that if the people who made the site were there long enough to build and use one hearth, one roasting pit, and ten other pits, they were there long enough to prepare and eat several meals. However, if plant leaves were eaten or if seeds were already ground to be used for cakes or gruel, they would not have been preserved. Only accidentally charred seeds and the charcoal for fueling cooking fires would have had a chance for preservation;

and even charred materials were subjected to eight thousand years of weathering and other forces that might destroy them before the archaeologists would recover them. Only the wood and kindling charcoal was actually preserved (Box 2-5).

The laboratory analyses helped the archaeologists piece together a general picture of when and how site D:11:3063 had been used (Figure 2-14). The **radiocarbon analysis** indicated conclusively that the site was occupied approximately eight thousand years ago, before pottery was invented in the New World and before plant domestication and cultivation. At that time, people survived by collecting plants and hunting small and large game. They lived in small groups and moved, either seasonally or more often, to places where plants and game were plentiful.

The hearth and roasting pit indicated to the archaeologists that some food preparation took place at the site. The roasting pit might have been used for preparing collected plant foods, such as agave or yucca, or for drying meat before it was transported back to a home site. The other ten pits were something of a mystery; they might have been basketry supports, trash pits, or any number of things. The absence of plant remains other than wood and kindling charcoal and of animal bones might mean that no plants were collected and no animals were hunted at site D:11:3063. However, the large number of pits suggested that people camped for longer than

overnight and used the site as a temporary base for foraging or hunting. If so, no evidence of those activities has been preserved.

Figure 2-14. Very old sites may yield little material with which to date the site. Here archaeologists collect scattered bits of charcoal that will be sent to a radio-carbon lab for analysis and dating.

MAY, 6000 B.C.

The winter had been hard, and the stored seeds and nuts collected the previous summer and fall were nearly gone. Although it was late spring, there was frost almost every night and snow was not uncommon. This was always the leanest time of year; stored foods were nearly depleted, and the subfreezing nights and occasional snows limited plant growth. In a few weeks, pigweed and goosefoot greens would be available to supplement the dwindling stores of seeds, pinyon nuts, and game, but in the meantime food was in short supply.

A small group, all members of one **extended family,** was preparing for a collecting and hunting trip. The family consisted of two brothers, their mates, and the seven-year-old daughter of the older couple.

In past years they had had good luck hunting deer in the open grasslands and sage flats about fifteen miles south of the winter camp. Yucca grew in profusion there within an easy day's walk of the hunting area. Deer meat could be dried and carried back to the winter camp; and while the men were hunting, the women could collect yucca fibers to be made into cordage.

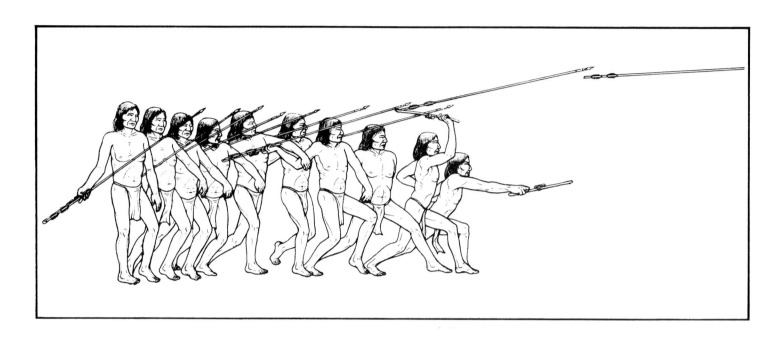

Figure 2-15 (above and far right). The atlatl, or throwing stick, and spear were used as a hunting tool before the invention of the bow and arrow. The atlatl increased the power behind the spear.

With luck they would find plants and small animals along the way and not need to dip too far into their limited winter stores, and they might bring back enough food to sustain themselves until the summer growing season.

Their preparations were simple and not time-consuming. The men checked their hunting tools: the atlatl and the spears propelled by the atlatl (Figure 2-15). One spear point was very worn and had been resharpened many times, so some pieces of obsidian and chert were packed along with the stone, bone, and antler tools used to make bifaces in case a new spear point was needed. The obsidian was the younger brother's contribution to the camp's resources. He had spent the previous year on a journey to the volcanic fields many miles south and west of their home territory. As a child he had wondered about the conical peaks that floated on the distant horizon, and he had heard stories of the abundant obsidian there to be had for the taking. While his parents were alive, they had discouraged both him and his brother from making the trip, but the old folks had died the year before, so nothing was stopping him. He and his brother had always dreamed of making the trip together, but his brother had long since married and had to stay with his family. The younger brother, however, was still eager to visit the volcanic fields and collect a supply of glassy obsidian for tool making. An equally important reason for making the trip was to visit the camps of other groups. He was in his late teens, and he wanted and needed a mate to share his life, but there were no girls near his own age other than his mar-

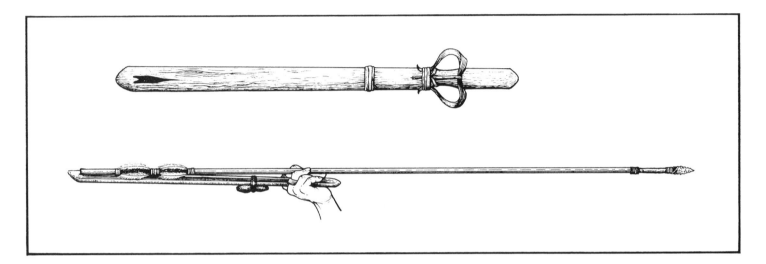

ried sisters, who lived nearby. If he wanted a mate, he was going to have to go look for one.

He had left in the early spring a year ago and had made it to the volcanic fields rather quickly. The return trip had been pleasantly delayed, however. At the western edge of the mesa, where Moenkopi Wash dropped onto the plain below, he had encountered his maternal uncle's camp. His uncle's daughter, thirteen or fourteen years old, had provided the incentive for him to stay there a while and help his uncle with the summer hunting. By early fall, he and his uncle's daughter had reached an understanding, and they requested permission to move from the uncle's camp to the boy's home camp. The uncle readily agreed; the boy was clearly an excellent hunter, and any sadness at his daughter's departure was tempered by the boy's gift of obsidian and the knowledge that there would be one less mouth to feed that winter. The young people had left the following morning, carrying the remaining obsidian, the girl's burden basket and digging stick, and a supply of food for the several-day journey to the boy's home camp. There they had been greeted with great relief by his older brother's family, who had been dreading the thought of a lonely winter. The younger brother and his new mate provided two additional able bodies for the fall hunting and seed gathering. And, almost as important, each of them had stories about distant places and different people to keep them entertained during the long and lonely winter.

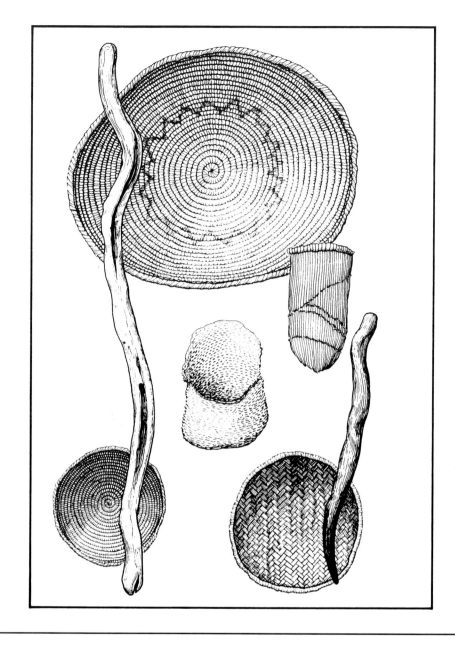

Figure 2-16. Baskets and digging tools like these might have been used by the Archaic peoples of Black Mesa.

The presence of the younger couple had been one of the few positive points during that long, hard winter. The winter's hardships had killed the older couple's second child, a three-year-old boy. With the lean winter diet, the older woman's milk had dried up. Although three years was not an especially early age for weaning, the child had had trouble digesting the seeds, nuts, and meat eaten by the group; weakened by diarrhea, he had died of fever in early winter. She suspected that she was pregnant again, but early pregnancy would not keep her from traveling with the group or from collecting plants or processing the meat. This would be her first long-distance foraging trip since her son had been born. While she was breast-feeding, she could not leave him for long periods of time, and he was unable to keep pace with the walking adults and older children. Her daughter was now able to travel with the foraging party and help collect and process food.

The women readied their baskets and digging sticks (Figure 2-16), and minimal quantities of seed cakes and dried meat were packed. They did not carry water because they expected to find it in the washes they would cross on their journey south. If there was no surface water, they would be able to tap groundwater by digging a shallow pit; the water table would be high following the winter snowmelt.

The group set out early the following morning. They reached their desti-

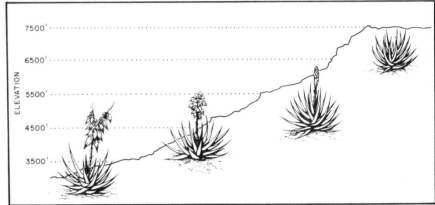

nation that same afternoon and set up camp in a spot overlooking a wash that flowed north through rolling, sage-covered hills. They had camped there before and were able to relocate the hunting camp by the hearth and pits left from previous trips. The hunting camp differed from their winter home, which was located under a small sandstone overhang (Figure 2-17). A wash bordered it as well, but there their source of water was the spring that flowed at the base of the cliff. The pinyon and juniper woodland surrounding their winter home was an excellent source of nuts and berries in the fall, but large game had been overhunted in the immediate vicinity. It was well worth the effort to travel the extra distance to increase their chances of encountering a large animal like a deer or an antelope. The women, who would help butcher and dry the meat, could also collect yucca and other low-altitude plants while they were waiting for the anticipated kill. Frosts at their winter home prevented new plant growth, but some plants might have already sprouted at this lower elevation. It would be especially nice to find a source of fresh greens (Figure 2-18).

Once camp was set up, the men left their burdens and reconnoitered the area for signs of game. They hoped to determine the feeding and watering patterns of the deer and to intercept their daily feeding round. The women set about making the camp inhabitable, cleaning out the hearth and scooping sand from holes for supporting their baskets. The little girl imitated the

Figure 2-17 (left). The protected winter camp of the site D:11:3063 occupants might have looked like another site on Black Mesa occupied about the same time. Site D:7:2085 was situated under the overhang of a sandstone cliff that faced southwest and would have provided shelter to its inhabitants during the long, cold Colorado Plateau winters.

Figure 2-18 (right). The same plants grow at different altitudes throughout Arizona. Because the growing season begins earlier at lower altitudes, plants growing there will germinate and fruit earlier than the same plants growing at higher elevations. If a site is situated within walking distance of a great elevation gradient, its inhabitants will have access to plants over a long period of time.

Figure 2-19 (left). Archaeologists often find finished tools because of a series of accidents. The projectile point on the right was broken during a hunting expedition. The prehistoric hunter made no effort to find the broken tip since it could not be reused for anything. However, the spear shaft with the point base still hafted to it was returned to the hunting camp. The broken base was removed and discarded, but the shaft was reused after a new point was hafted to it. The whole point, also found at site D:11:3063, was probably lost accidentally.

Figure 2-20 (right). The woman gathered baskets full of fresh greens for immediate consumption and to take back to the winter camp.

women and scooped out several holes of her own. The weather was ideal, warm with only a slight breeze, and the sky did not threaten rain or high winds, so they saw no need to construct a temporary shelter.

That evening after a meal of baby rabbits, which the men had taken from a burrow during their survey of the area, the group made plans for the morning. The brothers would continue to search for large game, and the women and the child would walk to the area known as Yucca Flat. There they would harvest yucca leaves, which they would transport back to the winter camp to be processed into cordage at a later time. They would also pick any greens found along the way for that evening's dinner. Their daily round would follow this pattern until the men killed a deer or an antelope. Then they would butcher the animal, dry the meat, and prepare the hide for their return to the main camp.

Two days passed in this way. The men determined that deer watered at the confluence of Juniper Grove and Yucca Flat washes in the early morning and then browsed in the open grasslands during the day before returning to the wooded uplands for the night. Unfortunately, one spear point was broken in an errant throw at a deer, so they spent the evening making a new point from some of the obsidian brought from the winter camp. They removed the base of the old point from the spear **shaft,** discarded it, and **hafted** the new point on the shaft. They left the broken tip where it fell; it was too small to be of further use (Figure 2-19).

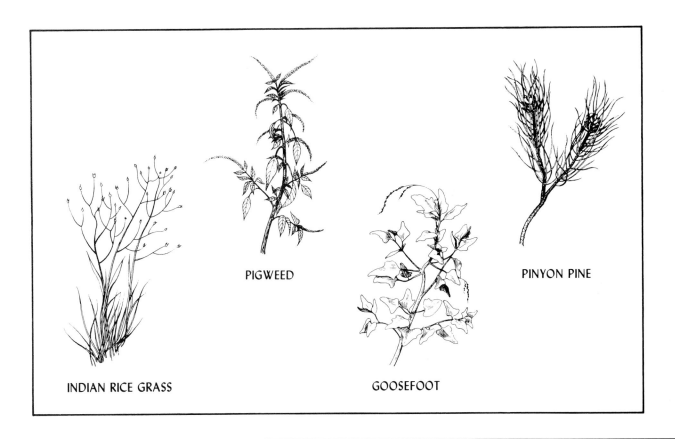

PIGWEED

PINYON PINE

INDIAN RICE GRASS

GOOSEFOOT

The women were pleased with the quantity of greens that had already sprouted at the lower elevation and looked forward to the welcome variation in their diet. They collected yucca leaves for cordage, and made plans to take a large basketful of greens back to their winter home (Figure 2-20). The women were disappointed that the sego lilies had not yet blossomed because the flowers would have been a tasty treat and the bulbs were excellent. They also collected a number of medicinal plants: cholla cactus roots to help cure diarrhea; yucca roots to use as a laxative; flax, bladderpod, and aster to aid in childbirth; and milkvetch to increase a mother's flow of milk. Although these plants were not used every day, the women found it reassuring to have them on hand (Figure 2-21).

On the morning of the third day the brothers were rewarded for their patience: they killed two deer at the watering place. This time their spears hit home, but one point was blunted on a bony shoulder.

Although they would return to their camp immediately, the men did not know whether the women were back from their gathering foray to help with the butchering. As a precaution against sour meat, they opened the stomach cavity of each deer and removed the innards. This also lightened the load that they would have to drag back to camp. As the men gathered up their hunting tools and started the return trip, they counted it a mixed blessing that the deer too had had a hard winter; they were easier to haul, but the meat would be lean, with almost no calorie-rich fat.

Figure 2-21. Parts of many plants were used by the Archaic period hunters and gatherers of northern Black Mesa.

Figure 2-22. The meat was butchered and dried to prevent spoilage and to ease the task of transporting it back to the winter camp.

The two men reached camp by early afternoon, before the women and the girl returned. They dug a large, shallow hole, and one began collecting juniper wood and large stones for a roasting pit, while the other started butchering the deer. The flake that had been used to open the stomach cavities had been dulled on the tough hide; although no longer useful for cutting hide or ligaments, it was ideal for separating the hide from the carcass. They pulled the flesh from the carcass in muscle sections, following the grain of the meat, and using sharp stone flakes cut these long sections across the grain into more manageable pieces. Luckily the day was dry and warm; as the meat dried, a hard film formed that protected it from flies. The men then placed the pieces on a rack to dry over the low fire (Figure 2-22).

The women returned to camp in time to do most of the butchering while the men told them different versions of how they stalked and killed the animals. By evening the deer had been butchered, and the family enjoyed a meal of fresh liver, bone marrow, and greens.

While they discussed their morning plans, one of the men resharpened the butchering tools and the blunted spear point. He discovered that the point had been resharpened so many times that there wasn't enough of it left to be useful, so he tossed it aside. They decided to return to the winter camp the following morning. They had accomplished what they intended. With luck the food they had accumulated would last until the growing season began at their winter camp or until they moved on for the summer.

BASKETMAKER

CHAPTER 3

Box 3-1. Archaeologists identify prehistoric sites by looking for things the occupants left behind when they left their homes. Often, because of the hundreds or thousands of years since abandonment, much of the most obvious evidence has deteriorated or disappeared completely. Organic remains, such as wooden and mud houses, wooden or bone tools, and garbage, disappear—often without a trace. Burned, or carbonized, organic remains may leave some evidence if they have not been blown or washed away. For many of the sites on northern Black Mesa, the most abundant remains are broken pottery and shaped stone blocks from tumbled-down masonry rooms. But there were no such remains on this site.

Box 3-2. After surveying in an area for some time, an archaeologist becomes aware of what the ground looks like when it is undisturbed. Specific kinds of vegetation grow in each type of soil; if the "wrong" vegetation is growing, it may mean that the soil's composition was altered by people dumping garbage in the area or breaking up the underlying soil.

Box 3-3. Different kinds of stone outcrop at different elevations, and pieces of stone were naturally found near to or downhill from their outcrops. Sandstone found away from its source must have been carried either by natural erosional forces, like wind or water, or by people.

Figure 3-1 (top). Soil that is a different color or texture from the surrounding soil often indicates human activity. Here the dark circular stain was formed when windblown sand and charcoal filled the depression left by a collapsed pit structure.

Figure 3-2 (bottom). The many equally sharp edges on this stone resulted when several flakes were removed all at one time; this could only have been done by humans. The tool was found on the surface of site D:11:449.

SURVEY: SEPTEMBER 27, 1975

Something was "wrong" (unnatural) with the ground. The survey crew chief called out to the other crew members to stop for a few minutes while he rewalked the surface to see if he could figure out what was so unsettling (Figure 3-1; Boxes 3-1, 3-2). He noticed chunks of gray siltstone and remembered that he had walked over an outcrop of similar stone about fifty yards south of this spot. Since he had climbed a low rise after leaving the outcrop and before stopping here, it was unlikely that the siltstone had washed to this location (Box 3-3). He stooped to examine one piece more closely and noticed that the stone had sharp, broken edges. What was unusual was that all the edges were equally sharp. If the stone had been naturally broken, some edges would be rounded by subsequent action of wind and water, while others would be sharp from recent breakage. The location of the stone and its sharp edges suggested that it had been brought here and that several pieces had been flaked from it all at one time. This could only be done by humans (Figure 3-2).

While he was mulling this over, he heard a call from another crew member who had found some chunks of fire-reddened sandstone and some dark soil that appeared to be a charcoal **stain.** Another person called their atten-

Figure 3-3. The partially dismantled hogan and the lithic debris suggest that this locale was attractive to both prehistoric Basketmakers and Navajos.

tion to some very small chips of white siltstone. There was no longer any doubt: this was definitely an archaeological site.

One crew member pointed out the partially dismantled Navajo **hogan** on the edge of the **scatter** of chipped stone (Figure 3-3). There was also a sheep corral just outside the scatter, east of the hogan. Although only chipped stone debris lay over most of the site, there were several prehistoric **potsherds** right around the hogan. The crew knew that many of the Navajos living on Black Mesa, like people everywhere, were curious about prehistoric peoples and had been known to collect relics from archaeological sites. This raised the possibility that all the artifacts had been collected by Navajos and brought here, which would mean that the dark, organically stained soil was from recent cooking fires, not from a prehistoric occupation.

The archaeologists were in a quandary about what to do. Clearly the Navajo hogan and corral were one site, but the chipped stone and potsherds suggested two other occupations. The white stone chips, pieces of white baked siltstone, were usually associated with the Basketmaker II period (Box 3-4).

They decided to treat the area as two sites, one Navajo and one **preceramic.** They felt that the small number of potsherds and the many different time periods to which they dated meant that they had probably been

Box 3-4. Basketmaker II was a preceramic period more recent than the Archaic: Basketmaker II sites were generally occupied sometime between 300 B.C. and A.D. 200. The presence of the potsherds only added to the complexity because they might be the remains of yet a third occupation.

collected by the Navajo occupants of the site. However, the chipped stone was scattered over more than a thousand square yards and was probably the remains of a Basketmaker II occupation (Box 3-5).

The archaeologists drove a datum stake carved with the site number, D:11:449, into the ground at the approximate center of the chipped stone scatter. The site was located on a sage flat, and the ground rose gently on the north and south. There was little erosion, and the chipped stone artifacts covered a clearly definable area. They measured the distance from the datum stake of eight points—north, west, south, and east; northwest, southwest, southeast, and northeast—where the **artifact density** declined suddenly. Then they mapped the points on graph paper and connected them with lines to mark the site's boundaries. Within these bounds, the survey crew laid out a temporary grid of 4 × 4–meter squares, using long measuring tapes. This temporary grid was used to map the surface characteristics of the site and to establish **provenience** control for the collection of surface artifacts.

The archaeologists needed a **representative sample** of artifacts for dating the site and for determining the types of activities that took place there. Collecting everything would have generated a massive quantity of materials, far too much for the surveyors to carry in their backpacks. One way to sample the site was with a "grab sample" of whatever happened to catch

their eyes. But the surveyors knew that earlier studies on Black Mesa and in other areas had shown that grab samples often overrepresent brightly colored or unusual artifacts. Although they were interesting, such artifacts could not be used to reliably date or reconstruct all past activities at the site. So instead, the crew chief **randomly selected** ten 4 × 4–meter squares for surface collection. This sample would furnish enough artifacts to date the site and to make a preliminary assessment of the kinds of activities carried on there.

There were no visible signs of structures or features that could be absolutely assigned to the preceramic occupation. The surveyors saw a few charcoal stains that might be the remains of Navajo cooking fires or trash deposits, so they noted them on the map and filled out a form for the Navajo site, to which they assigned the number D:11:451.

The information recorded on the form for the prehistoric site, D:11:449, was scant. The surveyors described and mapped its location and made notes about the surrounding landscape, soils, and vegetation. The area of the artifact scatter was mapped, as were the locations of the hogan, the corral, and potsherds. In addition, they noted the questionable association of the Basketmaker II chipped stone with the more recent potsherds and the Navajo site (Figure 3-4).

Figure 3-4. The beautifully preserved baskets that gave the Basketmaker culture its name were found in dry caves. Such preservation is very unusual; most organic finds are more like these two-thousand-year-old basketry fragments found during excavations at a Black Mesa Basketmaker site like D:11:449.

Figure 3-5 *(left). Excavation equipment, food, and water were transported to the site every day.*

Figure 3-6 *(right). The site's surface was resurveyed prior to excavation, and a grid of 1 × 1–meter squares, marked by stakes, was established.*

EXCAVATION: JUNE 1983

The excavation crew unloaded their trucks (Figure 3-5), carried the equipment to the datum stake, and placed the lunch cooler and water in a shady spot under a couple of juniper trees. Most of them had never done archaeological work on Black Mesa. Under the direction of the crew chief, an experienced hand, they set the off-site datum and the north-south and east-west axes of the grid system. Once this was done, they laid a grid over the entire site, cleared it of brush, mapped it, and collected artifacts from its surface, tasks that kept them extremely busy (Figure 3-6).

The map of the surface verified that there was indeed a Basketmaker II site here. After the crew had cleared the brush from the lithic scatter, a pattern emerged: the historic site was in the east, and the chipped stone was primarily west of the hogan. The **ashpile** was just where Navajo ashpiles normally are: about thirty feet east of the hogan's door, which also faced east. There was one large area of dark soil northwest of the on-site datum. The archaeologists felt that it was prehistoric because of the location and because it looked much older than the ashpile; there was no charcoal present in the stain, only a grayish brown color probably caused by disintegrated charcoal.

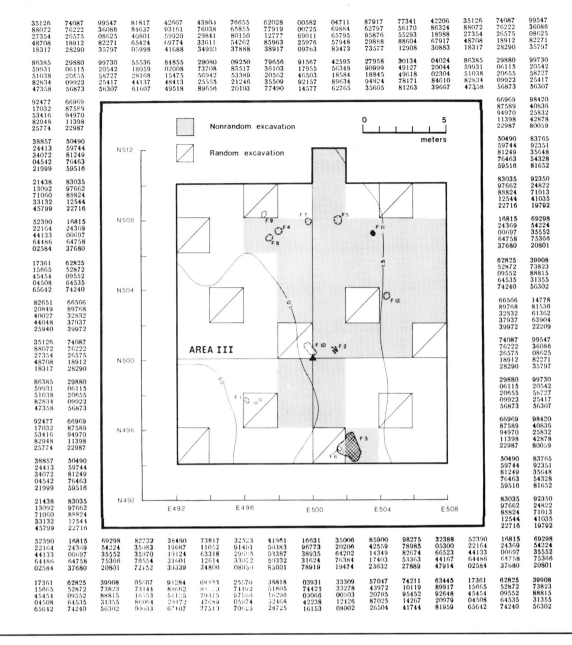

Figure 3-7. The map of the site's surface was used to divide the site into areas for excavation. Certain areas were totally excavated, but in others only a sample, randomly selected using a random number table, was dug.

Other than the stain and the chipped stone debris, little remained to suggest that prehistoric peoples had lived here. The potsherds surrounding the hogan were from many different types of broken pottery that had been made over a period of three hundred years. The excavators agreed with the surveyors that the potsherds had probably been collected and deposited by the inhabitants of the hogan. There were no other signs of a prehistoric occupation.

They divided the site into three areas for excavation. Area I included the section around the on-site datum and the dark soil. If any structures were on site D:11:449, they would probably be found there, so Area I was totally excavated. In Area II, which had a high density of chipped stone, one of every four 2 × 2–meter units was excavated. Area III included the northern and eastern portions of the artifact scatter that overlapped the Navajo site. Few artifacts had been found there, so only one of every six units was selected for excavation (Figure 3-7).

Because there were few signs on the surface to guide the archaeologists, they proceeded cautiously with the excavations. First they excavated the couple of inches of windblown sand covering the surface of Area I, recorded both the horizontal and the vertical provenience, and screened the soil through quarter-inch mesh. Then they bagged, labeled, and invento-

Figure 3-8 (left). The edges of earthen pit structures are located by trenching through the stain. In some cases archaeologists trying to excavate the fill from inside a structure or feature may unintentionally excavate into culturally sterile soil because there was no clear delineation between the fill and the surrounding soil. Doing so removes and destroys all evidence of the structure or feature.

Figure 3-9 (right). The profiles show a clear demarcation between the charcoal-stained fill and the clean, undisturbed soil.

Box 3-6. Sweeping clears away all loose sand from the ground surface so that differences in soil color and texture show up. Disturbed soils, such as the fill in a collapsed pithouse, are often softer and darker than the surrounding undisturbed soil. On a swept surface, soil filling a pithouse depression would become visible as an irregular oval or circular stain that was slightly lower and less smooth than the surrounding soil.

ried all the artifacts. Once the crew had removed the **overburden,** they swept the entire area with household brooms (Box 3-6).

Sweeping disclosed an irregularly shaped area with charcoal staining that contained many burned pieces of sandstone. The area was too large—almost twenty-five feet across—and too strangely shaped to be a structure. The excavators were mystified about its function. They could excavate the area by following the contact line between the fill and the undisturbed soil, but this procedure would remove and destroy most of the feature. If they did not find out what the feature was by excavating it, they would have no other evidence to go on. As an alternative, they excavated two narrow perpendicular trenches through the stain (Figure 3-8). These trenches revealed clear soil profiles and left most of the fill intact.

The trench profiles showed a clear but uneven demarcation between the fill and the **culturally sterile soil** (Figure 3-9). Charcoal and burned sandstone were distributed throughout the fill. The archaeologists mapped the trench profiles and then proceeded to excavate three-quarters of the remaining fill in **natural levels**; the fourth quarter was left in place to provide **stratigraphic control.** They found three semicircular depressions that had been formed by a large number of smaller overlapping pits. Some artifacts were sieved from the fill, and some small animal bones were recovered. Since the excavators thought that the pits had probably been used

Figure 3-10. The layer of sandstone and charcoal was what was left of the structure's roof. The pithouse had burned, and the weakened roof supports had collapsed. The sandstone slabs were probably laid much like shingles over the wood and earthen roof.

for preparing plant foods, they were scrupulous about taking several soil samples for flotation and analysis.

A second stained area appeared immediately south of the first, but it was circular and about twelve feet in diameter, just the right shape and size for a structure. Because they knew it would be difficult to recognize the floor in an earthen structure, the excavators also placed a trench through this stain so that they could look at it in profile. The trench profile disclosed a one-foot zone of dark brown sand over a layer of burned sandstone and carbonized wood. Several large sandstone slabs separated these two layers. Just below the sandstone-and-charcoal layer the excavators found culturally sterile soil.

The excavators felt that the sandstone-and-charcoal layer was made up of the remains of the structure's burned and collapsed roof (Figure 3-10). The crew cleared the **roof-fall** from the structure so that the floor could be exposed. They recovered several projectile points, beads, a pendant, sixteen human teeth, and human bone from the fill between the floor and the roof-fall. Several broken **manos** and **metates** were found on the floor, but there were no features there. The excavators thought that the large sandstone slabs they found in the fill and on the floor had been used to line the walls or had been placed on the roof, much like shingles, to protect it.

They found the edges of another structure-size stain overlapping the

Figure 3-11 (left and right). *Ramadas provided shade from the sun during the warm season. Today Navajos use similar structures that they roof with freshly cut juniper boughs.*

southwestern portion of Area I and one of the randomly selected units in Area III. It was a shallow pithouse, two feet deep and approximately twelve feet wide, which had also burned. They collected eight tree-ring samples, probably roof beams, from its fill, and they found five postholes, a hearth, and five other pits in the floor. Since the five pits had no characteristics that would suggest how they had been used, the archaeologists took flotation samples from each with hopes that preserved seeds or charcoal might provide some clues. **Groundstone,** chipped stone, and a small sandstone disc were also found on the floor.

They found a final structure in the southeastern corner of the site. Unlike the other two, this one was defined by postholes encircling three features (Figure 3-11). The features were all shallow pits, and the excavators had little idea of their functions. The size of the structure, approximately ten feet across, and the postholes suggested that a brush roof had been supported by six posts. Navajos use similar structures, called **ramadas,** today on Black Mesa as protection against the summer sun.

Twelve features were clustered just north of the ramada; one was a **storage pit,** but functions for the other eleven could not be determined. Six more features were grouped on the east side of the ramada, along with many pieces of burned sandstone. One was a **bell-shaped pit** (a pit whose opening is smaller than its basin), and five were shallow basins lined with

slightly oxidized soil (Box 3-7). The soil in these pits was only slightly discolored and not hard-baked. The excavators surmised that the heat source had been less intense than direct firing; perhaps rocks had been heated elsewhere and then placed in the basins. The absence of charcoal in these features supported the interpretation.

The archaeologists found two clusters of bell-shaped pits in the area between the two pithouses and the ramada. They also uncovered parts of five pits, which were detected as circular charcoal stains, in randomly selected units, and they excavated adjacent units to trace out these stains. In total, they found thirteen pits, all dug into the hard subsoil and all with burned (oxidized) walls. In the fill of several pits they found sandstone slabs, presumably used as lids or covers. A sandstone slab lined the floor of one of the pits. The crew collected soil samples from all of the pits for flotation and screened chipped stone, groundstone, beads, and animal bones from the fill. These materials had probably washed into the pits after site D:11:449 had been abandoned.

As excavations came to a conclusion, the archaeologists were somewhat puzzled. By Basketmaker II standards, the site had not been difficult to excavate. The fact that both pithouses had been destroyed by fire made their remains easily distinguishable. The preserved roof beams meant that there was plenty of material for dating the wood used in construction, either by

Box 3-7. Oxidation occurs when the soil comes into contact with a heat source, turning the soil red or orange. Hearths were frequently oxidized to bright red or orange, and their clays were hardened or fired.

tree-ring dating or, more likely, by radiocarbon dating. The ramada, its associated features, and the storage pit area had been relatively easy to find and to excavate. All had been built and used in ways familiar to archaeologists; all left remains that survived the two thousand years between the abandonment of the site and its rediscovery and excavation. In addition, none of the structures or features were built over others, so all were relatively intact.

All this suggested that a small group of people, perhaps two families, had inhabited site D:11:449. The large number of bell-shaped storage pits implied that the people planned to stay there for quite some time. If the pits had been used to store grains like corn or wild plant seeds, they would have accommodated enough food for several months. The pithouses implied occupation during the winter season, and the ramada, its associated features, and the storage pits pointed to occupation during and following the summer growing season. All this indicated that at various times site D:11:449 had been inhabited during most or all of the year.

It was the lack of consistency in Black Mesa Basketmaker II sites that was so frustrating; each was unique. And to make matters worse, the surface remains gave little indication of what would be found underground. During the later Puebloan period there were clear relationships between what was on a site's surface and what was found below, but this was not so for Basket-

maker II sites. The archaeologists felt that they had added to the overall picture of life on Black Mesa during this period, but at times they had the discouraging feeling that they would have to excavate every Basketmaker II site they found if they were ever to understand exactly what these people were doing here almost two thousand years ago.

Figure 3-12. Cores, waste flakes, and finished tools were found at site D:11:449. This means that tools were made, used, broken, and discarded there. But given the large number of waste flakes, there were very few tools.

ANALYSIS: JUNE–AUGUST 1983

The lithic specialists were amazed at the similarities among the artifacts found on site D:11:449. Of 8,256 pieces of chipped stone, only 231 were tools. The rest were waste flakes from tool production. Many of the artifacts were the small, flat chips characteristic of biface production; yet very few finished tools were actually found on the site (Figure 3-12). This could mean that finished tools, such as projectile points, were used, broken, and discarded at some place away from site D:11:449. However, if projectile points were broken during use, there should have been more broken bases. The Basketmakers would have recovered their dart shafts and returned them to their **base camp** for refurbishing. Presumably, they would then have removed the broken points from the shafts and discarded them.

Another curious aspect of the chipped stone **assemblage** was the relatively few causes of edge damage on the tools. Different kinds of materials,

Box 3-8. Siltstone is layered with the sandstones and coal deposits that form Black Mesa, and siltstone outcrops occur at numerous places throughout the area. Siltstone occurs in many colors—notably white, yellow, red, and gray—depending on the trace minerals found with it. Some of these deposits have been baked by natural fires in the coal seams. Contact with high temperatures improves the quality of siltstone for making chipped stone tools. In much the same way as intense heat changes the physical characteristics of clay when it is fired, the coal-seam fires improve the grain and fracture quality of the siltstone. Instead of crumbling, the baked siltstone fractures evenly, with sharp edges.

Figure 3-13 (above). Naturally coal-fired siltstone outcropped only a few hundred yards from site D:11:449. Chipped material was scattered over the hillside, indicating that the outcrop had been used as a quarry. Stone from this source was used to make many of the tools found at the site.

Figure 3-14 (above, right). Some archaeologists think that manos held in one hand and basin-shaped metates were used to crush and grind many different kinds of seeds.

Figure 3-15 (far right). The same archaeologists argue that corn was ground using more specialized, efficient tools: mealing bins or trough metates and two-hand manos.

like wood or animal hides, cause distinctive damage to the working edges of stone tools. So the patterns of edge damage, in combination with the absence of finished tools, suggested that despite its size (large for a Basketmaker II site), only a limited number of activities took place at the site. Perhaps the Basketmakers farmed near site D:11:449 and processed and stored their cultivated foods there but moved elsewhere to hunt and to gather wild plants.

White baked siltstone is an especially good raw material for chipped stone tools, and the Basketmakers used it in preference to other colors of siltstone (Box 3-8). It was the most common raw material used on site D:11:449, but gray baked siltstone was also found in unusually large quantities.

The analysts noted that considering the amount of gray baked siltstone, there were very few tools. Cores, which are chunks of stone from which flakes have been removed, were very common. This was unusual because stone is heavy and as little as possible was carried from the quarry to the place where it was made into a finished tool. The many large gray baked siltstone cores hinted that a quarry was nearby.

On the suggestion of the laboratory analysts, the field crew rechecked the area of the siltstone outcrop recorded by the surveyors. Siltstone outcrops are common, but the analysts suspected that this one was a quarry

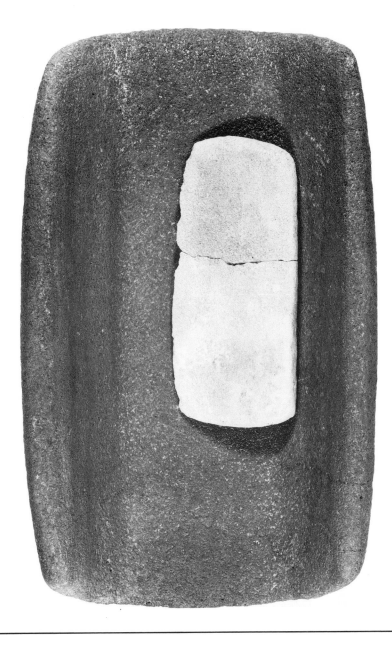

Box 3-9. Some archaeologists argue that small manos, gripped with one hand, were used to crush and pulverize seeds from noncultivated plants, whereas two-hand manos were used to make flour from corn. Their logic suggests that a diet of wild plants included several plant parts from many different plants. Availability would determine the diet; people would collect and consume whatever they could find in a specific place at the time they were there, but no single plant would dominate the diet. Some plant parts would have to be crushed before they could be eaten; others would be ground. A generalized tool, one that could be used for both crushing and grinding, would be more useful in this context than a tool that could be used only for grinding.

If people were growing a domesticated crop like corn, however, it probably played an important part in their diet throughout the year, to the exclusion of foods previously collected and eaten. Since people had to plant and tend their fields, there was no longer time to forage for wild plants. Their diet became simplified because of the emphasis on corn; as a result, food preparation tools could be specialized for use on corn. Written accounts of modern or historic Native Americans who consume large quantities of corn suggest that women spend many hours each day grinding corn into flour for that day's meals. It makes sense that people would try to develop the most efficient tools possible to minimize the time spent on this task.

Archaeologists view the change from one-hand to two-hand manos as a trend toward increased grinding efficiency. The grinding surface of a two-hand mano is twice as big as that of a one-hand mano, and two hands apply twice the force.

At the same time that two-hand manos replaced one-hand forms, metates changed from basin to trough to slab forms. The same argument, the need for increased efficiency, is used to explain this shift. However, sensible as this argument seems, there is little direct evidence to support it. The introduction of corn to the Basketmakers' diet does not mean that they ceased to eat other plant foods. And two-hand manos might have been used on wild seeds as well as on corn. The actual pattern is probably not as clear-cut as archaeologists would like to believe.

One procedure that helps to resolve the question of mano function is the pollen wash. A weak acid is poured over the tool's utilized surface. If plant pollen was left on that surface, it is carried off in solution with the acid. The acid solution is then examined under a microscope, and the pollen grains identified by a palynologist. Often the pollen collected this way was abraded by the mano and the metate. This mechanical damage is direct evidence that the pollen was deposited on the stones when seeds were ground into flour. Pollen from many plants, including corn and noncultivated species, has been found on manos and metates from northern Black Mesa sites.

(Figure 3-13). Sure enough, when they closely examined the loose rocks that lay downslope from the outcrop, they found that many of the pieces had been flaked. It appeared that the occupants of site D:11:449 were collecting the gray baked siltstone and making it into tools. The large amount of waste flakes and the small number of finished tools indicated that the tools were taken away after they were made.

The excavation crew collected eighty-six pieces of groundstone that had been used to grind corn and other seeds into flour. Five metates (the large flat grinding slabs), nine small manos (hand stones used with a one-hand grip), and sixteen large manos (used with a two-hand grip) were among the tools analyzed (Figures 3-14, 3-15; Box 3-9).

Soil is very important to archaeologists. Different kinds of soils and their relationships to one another tell them a great deal about how a site was built and used and what happened to it after it was abandoned. Most of site D:11:449's structures and features left only earthen remains. The two pithouses were bowl-shaped depressions dug into the soil; the ramada was a shallow depression ringed with postholes; the features ranged from hemispherical to globular holes. All in all there was very little evidence to suggest how these things had been used.

Some of the features were filled with charcoal and ashy soil and were

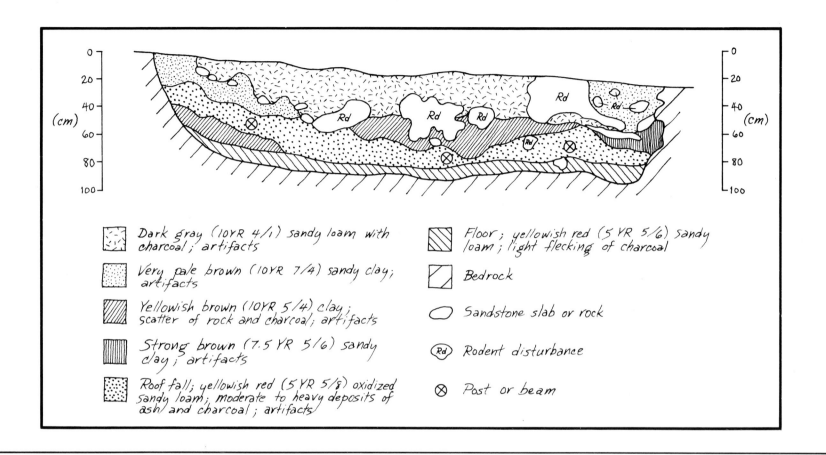

Dark gray (10YR 4/1) sandy loam with charcoal; artifacts

Very pale brown (10YR 7/4) sandy clay; artifacts

Yellowish brown (10YR 5/4) clay; scatter of rock and charcoal; artifacts

Strong brown (7.5YR 5/6) sandy clay; artifacts

Roof fall; yellowish red (5YR 5/8) oxidized sandy loam; moderate to heavy deposits of ash and charcoal; artifacts

Floor; yellowish red (5YR 5/6) sandy loam; light flecking of charcoal

Bedrock

Sandstone slab or rock

Rd Rodent disturbance

⊗ Post or beam

Figure 3-16. Archaeologists "read" soil profiles to determine the context of artifacts and samples. It is very important to distinguish items found on floors from those washed or blown into a structure after it was abandoned.

Box 3-10. The particles that compose fill are usually small, having been carried by wind or water. However, small pieces of charcoal and some artifacts from various sources are also blown or washed into the depressions. So a feature's or a structure's fill is made up of whatever was left there at its last use and the materials washed or blown in after it was abandoned. Although both types of materials are important, it is critical to distinguish between the two during analysis. Artifacts and samples are carefully labeled, and their contexts—either "fill" or "floor contact"—are written on the tag. Artifacts and samples taken from contact with a floor or the bottom of a feature are especially important in determining how a structure or feature was used and what it was.

almost certainly hearths. Most of these basins also had fire-reddened and -hardened soils around their edges. Both of the pithouses had layers of burned roof-fall above their floors. But even though this indicated that the depressions had been roofed, it said little about how the structures had been used.

The structures and the features (other than the hearths) were filled with charcoal-flecked soil. The archaeologists could distinguish the soil inside the features from the surrounding undisturbed soil because it was browner and less densely packed and because of the charcoal flecking. The structures and features had filled up over the years with soils carried by wind and water from the surface of the site (Figure 3-16; Box 3-10).

Soil to be used for pollen and flotation samples was collected from the fill and from contact with the floor during the excavation process. If there were no artifacts or preserved organic materials to show how the feature or structure had been used, and there rarely were any, the microscopic pollen and plant remains would provide the only information. The excavators also collected samples from the hearths; even though their function was obvious, the types of woods used as kindling and fuel told much about the shrubs and trees that grew around site D:11:449 while it was occupied.

The plant analysts found juniper and pinyon charcoal in all the samples. Site D:11:449 was surrounded by a pinyon and juniper woodland, and its

Figure 3-17. Most archaeological evidence of agriculture is indirect. Because organic remains are so infrequently preserved, the tools for processing them are often the only evidence for corn agriculture. Manos and metates for grinding grain and ceramic vessels for cooking it are frequently the only archaeological remains that suggest the presence of agriculture. However, these tools could also have been used to process and cook other kinds of foods.

Direct evidence comes from another source. Early southwesterners were frugal; once the corn was removed from the cobs, the cobs were dried and used for kindling. This carbonized the cobs, sections (cupules) of which were later recovered by archaeologists through flotation techniques. However, the recovery of cupules tells archaeologists only that corn was present; it sheds no light on how much corn was grown and eaten.

wood provided fuel for cooking and heating. Most of the samples contained small pieces of corn kernels that had disintegrated when the dried cobs were burned as kindling (Figure 3-17). They found grass seeds, Indian ricegrass, goosefoot, kochia, and beeweed seeds in other samples. These are annuals, and their seeds would have been ripe and ready for collection during the summer and into the autumn.

Over a hundred wood samples were taken and submitted to the Tree-Ring Laboratory at the University of Arizona for **dendrochronological** dating (Box 3-11). Most of the wood was from roof-fall layers in the two pithouses, but some came from the bottoms of the bell-shaped storage pits. Unfortunately, the tree-ring specialists were not able to date any of the samples, and none of them could be used to assess whether the pithouses and pit features from which they came were all built at the same time.

Forty-two other wood samples were taken for possible radiocarbon dating. These samples were not submitted until the dendrochronological results were received because radiocarbon dating is much less precise and much more expensive than tree-ring dating. Only five samples were submitted for radiocarbon analysis. Results ranged from 390 B.C. to 20 B.C., with error terms of sixty or seventy years. The analysts realized that there is always the problem of determining the relationship between the wood being dated and the structure or feature that it came from. However, one of

Box 3-11. Tree-ring dating is the most precise chronometric method available to southwestern archaeologists. Each year trees produce a growth ring. If the year was wet, with much moisture available for growth, the ring will be wide; if little moisture was available, the ring will be narrow. Annual rainfall in the Southwest has been so variable, and the pattern of variation so distinctive, that the ring patterns can be used to determine the year that a tree died.

the site D:11:449 samples, which dated to 390 B.C. ± 70 years, was taken from corn collected from the hearths near the ramada. Since corn is a cultivated annual plant, its direct association with those features is clear. The analysts thought that given the wide range of dates, there were perhaps two or more occupations of site D:11:449.

The excavations and analyses confirmed what the surveyors had suspected, that site D:11:449 dated to the Basketmaker II period. The relatively few structures indicated that a small number of people, perhaps two or three families, lived there. The large quantities of chipped stone debris, especially the gray baked siltstone, were left over from tool production. Because there were so few finished tools found on the site, the archaeologists thought that the Basketmakers probably carried them away and used them elsewhere. Corn, nondomesticated plants, and the groundstone tools implied food cultivation, collecting, and processing. The numerous storage pits were somewhat mysterious but indicated the capacity for storage of large quantities of food or other materials.

In some ways, site D:11:449 was like other Black Mesa Basketmaker II sites: the remains seemed incomplete, as if the occupants spent part of the year doing other things in other places. However, the storage pits and the gray baked siltstone quarry were unique.

LATE SUMMER, 325 B.C.

Last winter had been cool and wet. The moisture had seeped into the soil, and soil conditions were now ideal for the corn and squash and for the weedy annuals that grew in their fields and around their homes. They had been planting corn for as long as the man could remember, and his father and grandfather had survived off the land in the same way.

During good years, there might be enough game and wild edible plants to support him and his family. Frequently, however, conditions were not good, and then the wild plants produced poorly and game was in short supply. They could not count on foraging long distances from their home during bad years: their neighbors had staked claims to those territories, although they lived several miles away. He had heard of places that were still so sparsely inhabited that people could wander freely, hunting and collecting, without regard for others. But that was not possible here, and had not been for generations. He knew from experience that it was wise to plant the corn just in case. It could always be stored, and even if they did not need it for survival, the corn provided welcome variation in their often monotonous winter diet of dried foods.

They did not actively tend the fields after planting (Figure 3-18). If there were elderly people or young children who were not otherwise occupied,

Figure 3-18. The Basketmakers probably did not weed their fields after planting. The "weeds" were almost as valuable to them as the corn and squash intentionally planted there.

they might spend their days and possibly even nights in the fields scaring away birds and rodents. Children hunted, and the elderly set nets or snares to kill the rabbits and hares that were attracted to the young plants. But the fields were not weeded. The "weeds," like pigweed and goosefoot, were the same plants collected for greens and seeds. They grew in the fields and in other areas where the ground had been recently disturbed, and since they were good food sources, they were left to grow along with the corn and squash that were intentionally planted. If there was enough water and no frost, everything flourished.

He thought that his family (his mate, teenage son, and ten-year-old daughter) would probably once again spend the winter at this site. His younger brother had not yet mentioned his family's plans, but it was likely that both families would winter together. The two families had homes here and planted fields nearby. But they could stay in other places with other relatives as well. If things went poorly for them this summer, they could always pack up food and supplies and move in with relatives for the winter. Similarly, these relatives would come stay with him and his brother if they fared poorly in any given year. Sharing was necessary for survival, and it made him feel good to help others, knowing that he could rely on them if he had to.

Figure 3-19. Pithouses (shown here in cross section) were small and cramped, but very warm. They were probably used only during cold or wet weather.

Their settlement consisted of two shallow pithouses with low, cribbed-log roofs that were used by each family during the cold winter months (Figure 3-19). Everyone preferred being outdoors, so the small pithouses were used as little as possible. His family crowded together indoors only during stormy weather. When that happened, he made new spear points and repaired his hunting tools, his mate prepared food and wove furs together to make blankets, and they all told stories to pass the time spent in confinement.

During the winter, he made and repaired tools. One of the things he liked best about this location was its closeness to an outcrop of good gray baked siltstone. The gray siltstone was not as good for chipping as the white stone, but it was abundant and nearby, so he need not worry about using up limited supplies. Whenever he ran out of stone, he could just walk over the hill and get some more; the weather was rarely so bad that he could not make it to the quarry. Chipping stone into tools had helped him pass many winter days that otherwise would have been spent in idle boredom.

The families also had a ramada, which was used during warmer weather. Fewer people were at the site on any given day during the late spring, summer, and fall. Instead, everyone who was able worked in the fields, collected plants, and hunted. By late summer their thoughts turned to pre-

Box 3-12. The storage pits were dug into previously undisturbed soil to the depth of the digger's arm plus the digging stick. These pits had narrow openings that were easy to seal with a sandstone slab or two; but a few inches below the ground's surface, they flared out into a sphere. After finishing a pit, the digger filled the hole with dry tinder and torched it. Insects and larvae were killed by the searing heat, and the fire also hardened the pit's walls. This single step eliminated insect pests that might otherwise feast on the stored foods, and discouraged burrowing rodents by creating a fired-wall barrier.

paring enough food to last through the winter. During late summer and autumn, the ramada became the focus of activity; the women fueled low fires all day long and parched corn and other seeds for storage.

FALL, 325 B.C.

The season's early promise had been fulfilled. The soil had retained enough moisture from the melting winter snows to sustain the germinating seeds through the dry months of late spring and early summer. The summer thunderstorms started in July, as hoped, providing a necessary additional source of water after the soil lost the last of the snowmelt to evaporation.

All of the plants had flourished, and everyone who was able gathered seeds, competing with the birds and rodents for the bounty. The harvesters worked in the planted fields first, collecting the corn, squash, and edible weeds that grew in profusion there. Since the fields were close to their homes, all their time was spent collecting food; none was wasted searching for productive patches of plants or hauling back the harvested food. Only when the fields were harvested and gleaned would they move farther and farther from home, foraging for food until the weather made travel unsafe or impossible or until there was no more food.

Figure 3-20. The women parched the seeds before storing them. Unparched seeds might rot or mold and would not store for as long as the dried ones.

The women had to prepare the seeds for storage. If the seeds were not properly dried, they might rot or mold and become inedible. The women kept low fires burning constantly near the ramada. Chunks of sandstone were heated, and when they were hot, the women raked them from the coals to form a very hot, level surface. Then they placed seeds in a single layer on flat parching trays made of tightly woven basketry. They held the trays over the heated stones and tossed the seeds gently to expose them completely to the drying heat (Figure 3-20).

They ate some of the seeds immediately. Others they stored in deep earthen pits (Box 3-12). Each pit held several bushels of produce—enough calories to sustain an individual for several weeks. They had had to excavate several new pits to store all the corn and other seeds harvested this year. However, they all knew from unpleasant experience that they might not survive the winter and early spring on seeds and grain alone. They also needed meat protein and fat (Box 3-13).

The two brothers had completed their contribution to the harvest, and now it was up to the women to finish preparing the harvested corn and seeds for winter storage. The days were still clear and warm, but frosty nights hinted of cold weather to come. The conditions were ideal, and since they were no longer needed in camp, the men decided to go on a hunt.

The Basketmakers were not the only Black Mesa inhabitants to benefit

Box 3-13. Although the Basketmakers might not have had specific terms for it, they knew that something was missing nutritionally from the corn and seeds they collected. Lysine, one of the essential amino acids, occurred in insufficient amounts in their stored seed. Nine hundred years later, inhabitants of the area would also cultivate beans, which provided the necessary lysine. In Basketmaker times, however, beans were not yet known in the Southwest, and the Basketmakers had to rely on meat as their source of this necessary nutrient.

from the year's clement weather. Animals, too, relied on the grasses and shrubs that were now available in such abundance, and some—especially deer, mountain sheep, and antelope—were the preferred game of the Basketmaker hunters. There should be many animals now because most of the young would have survived the lean period of late spring. Furthermore, all of the animals should be fat from the lush fodder.

The men agreed to go north to the rim, where the rugged landscape was home to mountain sheep (Figure 3-21). They would also have the opportunity to check the status of the pinyon nuts. This was the second wet year in a row, so conditions were ideal for an excellent nut harvest. Often when they traveled along the mesa rim, they met hunters and foragers from the valley below. These meetings gave them a chance to exchange finished spear points and ornaments and to find out about conditions farther from home. If the harvest had gone as well in the valley as it had on the mesa, they might plan a get-together to celebrate.

The brothers and their sons made preparations for the trip. They inspected their spear throwers, sharpened the stone points that tipped the spears, and asked the women to pack food for one or two weeks. The women packed seed cakes and dried meat but reminded their men to eat the pinyon nuts instead if they were ready for harvest. The women also suggested that the men send one of the boys home with a message for

the women and girls to join them if the nut harvest near the rim was especially rich.

The trek to the rim country took less than a day, and it was only an additional half day's climb down the mesa's escarpment to the valley below. Several families lived in the valley, and although they saw each other only once or twice a year, the valley and mesa people were well aware of one another. It was important to learn how other groups had fared so that everyone would know who had food when times were rough.

The older brother's mate was born in the valley and spent her early years there. Even though by Basketmaker standards there were many people in the valley, there were few enough that she was related to all of them. When it came time for her to take a mate, she knew he would come from somewhere else, either from Black Mesa or from one of the groups of Basketmakers living north of the valley. All marriageable young adults eagerly anticipated their fall visits with other groups so they could look one another over.

After marriage, a young woman went to live with her husband because, as everyone knew, a man could not be expected to learn the ins and outs of a new hunting area. By the time a boy was old enough to hunt with the men, he knew every detail of the landscape for miles around his home and the habits of game within that landscape; it would take years to duplicate

Figure 3-21. The rugged terrain of Black Mesa's northern scarp was home to mountain sheep. Sheep bones found on Basketmaker sites were evidence that the Basketmakers had hunted the sheep.

Figure 3-22 (above and right). Basketmakers lived throughout the region, and signs of their occupations come both from "open" sites, like those on Black Mesa, and from "cave" sites. Many Basketmaker caves are located along the edge of Skeleton Mesa, just north of Black Mesa. The caves provided shelter from storms and insulated their inhabitants from temperature extremes. The same caves also protected the abandoned sites, preserving the deposits for archaeologists to find almost two thousand years later.

this knowledge in a new area. A woman, by contrast, could help more experienced women gather plants while she learned about a new area. It just made sense for the women to move to their husbands' homes.

All the Basketmakers in the region planted fields, foraged, and hunted during the summer and fall, just like the people of the mesa. However, there were differences in how individual groups lived, differences caused by local conditions. During the winter, generation after generation of valley people took shelter in large, shallow caves formed in the red sandstone cliffs by wind and water (Figure 3-22). Although mesa dwellers acknowledged that the caves were dry, they could not understand why people would choose to return to the same place year after year. Even stranger, the valley people buried their dead inside storage pits, sharing their cave homes with the spirits. The mesa dwellers chose to vacate a site whenever their homes deteriorated or whenever a better place beckoned. When one of them died, the body was left where the death took place, and the structure or site was no longer used. It might be reoccupied after a while, once the body had departed on its journey to the spirit world, but it was hard for the mesans to imagine living with the dead by choice. They knew, though, that there were more people in the valley and that there was no place for them to move.

The four started in midmorning and reached their destination at sunset. The pinyon trees on the rim were loaded with nuts, so the older brother

decided to send his son back to the main camp the following day with a message for the women and girls to join them. While waiting, the two brothers and the younger brother's son built a windbreak to shelter them all for the week or two that they would spend here hunting and collecting pinyon nuts. They gathered large logs from dead trees to form the basic shape. Smaller pieces of wood and brush shrubs were crammed in any open spaces to finish the shelter. The windbreak was U-shaped; the opening was to the northeast, facing away from the prevailing wind. There was a cooking and heating hearth in front of the entry. The shelter was not airtight, but it provided warmth and sufficient protection from the wind for the limited time that they would be here.

The older brother's son led the women and girls to the camp the afternoon of the second day. They brought parching trays and burden baskets to carry the nuts back to their winter home, but they had brought little additional food. They would all eat pinyon nuts and game while they were collecting and hunting.

The families divided into two work groups. The women and their daughters worked together collecting pinyon nuts and preparing them to be carried back home. They knocked the unopened pinyon cones from the trees and heated them to open the scales and remove the nuts (Figure 3-23). If the cones opened while they were still on the trees, the birds and rodents

Figure 3-23. The women knocked the unopened pinyon cones from the trees and then heated them to extract the nuts.

quickly ate the exposed nuts. By harvesting the cones before they opened, the women were able to gather what they needed before the birds and rodents had a chance at them.

The men and boys decided to try their hunting luck in the treeless area immediately south of the rim. They thought deer and antelope might browse there during the day, and they would be near enough to the rim to scout for signs of mountain sheep. They also thought that valley people might be hunting in the area and hoped to see signs of them.

The hunters started off in good spirits. The morning was cool, and there had been a light frost the night before. But the sky was clear and still, and the day promised to be warm. They moved through the pinyon and juniper trees in single file, trying not to disturb the morning stillness. After a short trek they entered an area favored by the valley people, and they kept their eyes open for footprints, broken vegetation, and other signs of their presence.

From a distance they heard the loud cawing and scolding of ravens. As the hunters grew nearer, they saw several of the large black birds just ahead. They hoped that the birds were feeding on the remains of an animal killed by valley hunters. If so, they could track the valley people from their kill and make contact with them.

The two boys broke away from the men and ran ahead to see what was attracting the ravens, but after a short time the men heard cries of horror

and dismay. The men quickened their pace to catch up with them. Both boys were accustomed to the sight of butchered game and carrion eaters; something else must be wrong to shock them so.

The men caught sight of the boys and were relieved that nothing was threatening them. Then, following the boy's line of vision, they saw the horrifying sight. They had found the camp site of a valley family, but they were all dead. Seven people—two men, a woman, a teenage girl, and three younger children—were sitting in and around a windbreak. Apparently they had died the night before. The remains of their meal suggested the cause of death. Pieces of mountain sheep scattered around the hearth looked to be several days old. The valley hunters had probably killed the sheep soon after they set up camp here. Although the meat did not look or smell especially bad, something in it must have poisoned the family.

The men knew what they had to do. They could not leave the bodies for the birds and other scavengers. They knew enough about the customs of the valley people to know that the bodies should be buried. There was an empty storage **cist** at the camp site, probably dug during an earlier camping trip. The men enlarged the pit so that it would accommodate the seven bodies. Then they placed the bodies in the grave along with the group's belongings, refilled the pit, and marked its location with a sandstone slab (Figures 3-24, 3-25).

Figure 3-24 (left). Seven men, women, and children were buried in the large pit along with their personal effects. The burial was unique for Black Mesa, where most human remains have been found inside structures or in trash middens. Pit burials are much more common in the Basketmaker caves located north of Black Mesa.

Figure 3-25 (right). The Basketmaker cist grave at site D:7:3141 during excavation.

Their unhappy task completed, the hunters returned to their women. They walked in silence, not wishing to voice their grief and fears. They had no heart to continue with their hunt. They were grateful that the valley dead were not the immediate family of the older brother's mate, but she would know the people, and their deaths would cause her grief.

The older brother guessed that the women and girls would want to stop their pinyon nut harvesting. That left them two options that he could see. They could return to their winter camp and mourn alone, or they could continue their journey north into the valley to bring word of the disaster to the valley people. Even as his mind formed the two thoughts, he discarded the first. Although the news would bring pain to the valley people, it would be better for them to know what had happened than to go through the winter worrying and wondering.

They would descend into the valley, and if the weather turned, they could winter with the valley people. If the weather continued clear and warm, they might return to their own winter homes. But their food was safely cached and would still be there come spring. If there was no pressing reason to return, they just might winter in the valley. Time would tell.

PUEBLOAN

CHAPTER 4

Figure 4-1. Although the Navajos are pastoralists and rely on their herds of sheep and cattle for subsistence, they also plant crops. Navajo cornfields are probably planted in the same places as prehistoric Anasazi fields.

SURVEY: AUGUST 5, 1980

The archaeological survey crew passed through the Begay settlement, avoiding the hogan and the lamb pens. The family had been friendly to them (two of the sons even worked on excavation crews), but the surveyors did not want to disturb any people or stock that might still be in camp. They filled out a site form and drew a sketch map of the settlement from a distance. Later they would ask permission to interview the Begays and to map their home, corrals, and outhouses with more precision.

Just past the Begay settlement the land dropped off into Moenkopi Wash. When the surveyors reached the crest, they stopped to take bearings and to determine the safest way down the slope. Two cornfields, probably planted by the Begays, were just west of their transect in the Moenkopi floodplain (Figure 4-1). The crew chief also noticed an interesting spot on a finger of land projecting south into the floodplain. It lacked vegetation and was covered with sandstone rubble. He checked the location on the topographic map and saw that the finger ridge formed a peninsula about the size of a football field, approximately seventy-five feet above the surrounding floodplain. Access to the ridge from above appeared to be relatively easy.

As the surveyors descended the slope, they discovered that the ridge was

barren because the stone rubble covering it kept plants from growing there and, more importantly, that the rubble was from ruined masonry rooms (Figure 4-2). Huge by Black Mesa standards, the site extended over the entire flat area of the ridge.

On the north edge of the site, they found an L-shaped arrangement of upright sandstone slabs and dark organically stained soil. About fifty feet southwest of the slabs, ceramic and chipped stone artifacts were densely scattered over soil that ranged from gray to black. The slabs marked two walls of a structure, and the concentration of artifacts and dark soil was what remained of a trash dump, or **midden** (Figure 4-3).

The surveyors walked southward over the site and found two more **rubble mounds.** The middle mound had upright slab walls, and the southernmost and highest of the three was a fifteen-by-forty foot heap of shaped sandstone blocks. South of the second rubble mound was a shallow depression (probably the remains of a buried pit structure) with a very large trash midden east of it. Near the third rubble mound the terrain dropped rapidly to the wash below.

It was unusual on Black Mesa to find a place close enough to a major wash to permit access to its floodplains for farming, yet high enough above the wash to be safe from seasonal flooding. Its nearness to fields and to the

Figure 4-2 (left). Because rubble from collapsed masonry rooms prevents trees and other large vegetation from growing, Puebloan sites often have little vegetation growing on them.

Figure 4-3 (right). The Puebloan occupants of Black Mesa deposited their trash in designated areas, which the archaeologists call middens. Middens are characterized by dark soil, discolored by ash and charcoal, and by many broken artifacts.

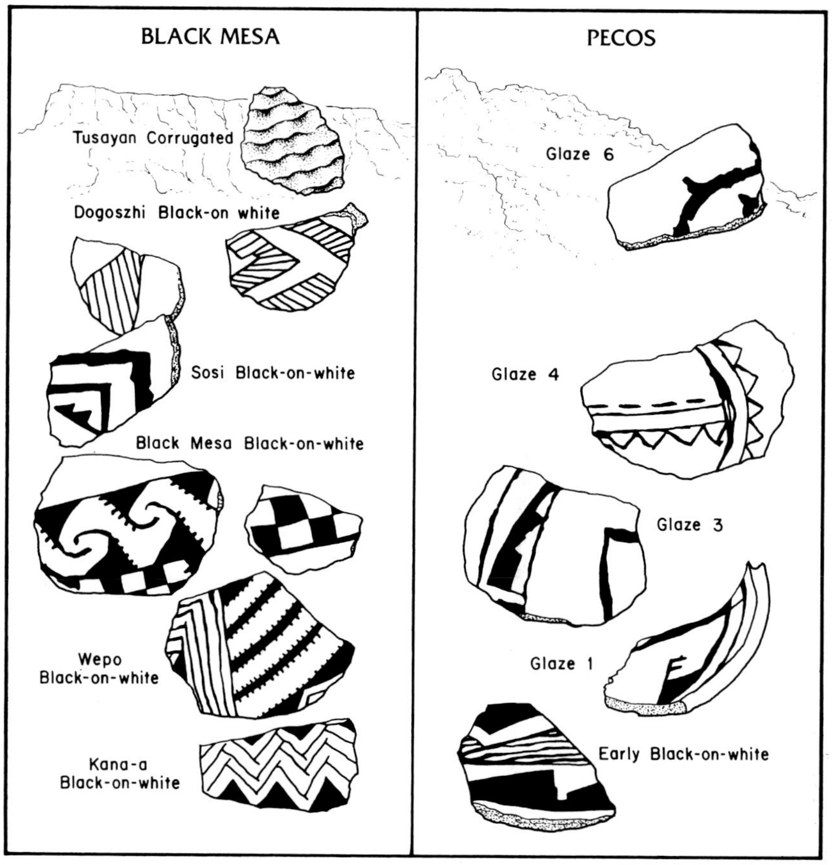

BLACK MESA	PECOS
Tusayan Corrugated	Glaze 6
Dogoszhi Black-on white	Glaze 4
Sosi Black-on-white	Glaze 3
Black Mesa Black-on-white	Glaze 1
Wepo Black-on-white	Early Black-on-white
Kana-a Black-on-white	

Figure 4-4. Ceramic artifacts from Anasazi sites like those on Black Mesa have been studied since the early 1900s. At the site of Pecos in New Mexico, for example, trash was deposited over long periods of time, with older deposits covered by successive layers of more recent deposits. Ceramic studies showed changes in decorative motifs from layer to layer. The different motifs could be dated relatively from oldest to youngest, just like the layers in which they were found. Similarly decorated ceramics from other sites were thought to date to the same periods as the ceramics at Pecos. Thus two sites with similar ceramics were presumed to have been occupied at approximately the same time. The introduction of tree-ring dating in 1929 allowed absolute dates to be assigned to many of the ceramic types.

Box 4-1. Usually artifacts will be evenly dense in the central, structural portion of a site but will decline in density away from the structures. A wide scattering of artifacts is often the result of erosion and does not represent cultural activities of interest to archaeologists.

pinyon and juniper woodlands to the south made the place ideal both for farming and for hunting and gathering.

The entire crew reconnoitered the area to determine the extent of the artifacts associated with the site. Because it was situated on a terrace above Moenkopi Wash, wind and water had eroded many artifacts down the slope toward the channel of the wash. These artifacts were not used to define actual site boundaries even though they came from the site (Box 4-1). Instead, the crew chief placed a datum stake in the approximate center of the building rubble and from there looked for changes in artifact density to determine the site boundary. Then the crew laid out a temporary grid, and squares were randomly selected for collection.

While they were collecting the artifacts, the archaeologists couldn't help noticing the many different kinds of potsherds. Some were gray and unpainted, others were painted with black on a white background, and still others had black and orange paint on a red background (Figures 4-4, 4-5).

Once they had collected the artifacts, the archaeologists marked the perimeter of the site with flagging tape. They made sure that the site map was complete and that the location was accurately marked on the topographic map. Then they packed up the bags of artifacts and clipboards and continued walking south on their transect.

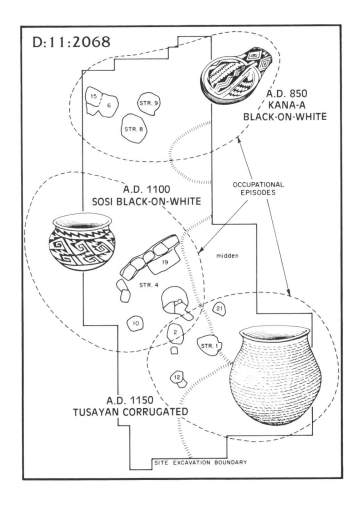

D:11:2068

A.D. 850
KANA-A
BLACK-ON-WHITE

15
6
STR. 9
STR. 8

A.D. 1100
SOSI BLACK-ON-WHITE

OCCUPATIONAL
EPISODES

19
STR. 4

midden

10
21
2
STR. 1
12

A.D. 1150
TUSAYAN CORRUGATED

SITE EXCAVATION BOUNDARY

EXCAVATION: MAY 30, 1981

Since the finger ridge was a prominent topographic feature, it was easy for the project supervisors to relocate the site. However, driving there was an entirely different matter. Peabody's coal haul road crossed the wash about one-half mile west of site D:11:2068, but access by truck from the haul road along the bottom of the wash to the site was difficult—and it was still the dry season. It would be extremely dangerous once the rains started in July. Many archaeologists needed to drive to site D:11:2068 every work-day for the entire summer. If the excavators had to walk and carry equipment, water, and food, precious time would be lost.

The supervisors mulled over these problems as they drove along the wash back to the coal haul road. If the Begays agreed and the Black Mesa Mine personnel were willing to help, a new road could be built south from the Begay settlement to the site.

The supervisors drove to the mine headquarters to confer with the mine superintendent and his assistant. They were intrigued by the problem and went back to site D:11:2068 with the archaeologists to investigate. All four walked the ridge from the wash bottom to the Begay settlement. After checking with the Begays, the mine superintendent radioed the mine head-

Figure 4-5. The surveyors knew that the types of ceramics found on Black Mesa sites were usually made between A.D. 850 and 1150, and they found most of them on this site. Potsherds in the vicinity of the northern set of structures generally dated to A.D. 850, those from the central and southern portions of the site to between A.D. 875 and 1150. This range of dates suggested that people had lived on the finger ridge continuously for three hundred years or more, or that at least three distinct sites had been built there over the years.

Figure 4-6. Access to site D:11:2068 was difficult even with no water flowing in the wash; it would be extremely dangerous once the rainy season started. A coal company grader was used to build a new road to site D:11:2068.

quarters and immediately dispatched a road grader to the site. Within the hour the problem was solved; not only was there a road to the site, but the grader operator also cleared and leveled a parking area for the trucks (Figure 4-6).

The excavators established an off-site datum and placed a grid system, but there was much work to do before excavation could begin. Areas of the site not littered with the sandstone rubble were covered with sagebrush. It obscured the ground and had to be cut and removed before the excavators could lay a grid, make a surface collection, and map all of the site. About twenty people worked on clearing the sage, with the added benefit of reducing the gnat population (Figure 4-7).

The artifact and structure maps were used to choose areas for excavation. Having observed the location of structures, trash middens, and **ceramic types,** the archaeologists thought that there had been at least three different villages occupied over a three-hundred-year period at site D:11:2068. The oldest occupation (Component I) was in the northern part of the site, the middle occupation (Component II) in the center, and the most recent (Component III) in the southern part. In each **component,** they chose sections with structural remains for complete excavation.

The archaeologists designated the large midden southeast of Components II and III a single sampling area even though it had probably been

Figure 4-7. Juniper gnats, whose bites raise itchy welts, always plagued the Black Mesa archaeologists from late May until the rains began in early July. The archaeologists developed a distinctive style of dress to combat the gnats. These insects live in the sage and other on-site plants, and clearing the brush destroyed their homes. Illustration by Rob Dunlavey, adapted for publication by Thomas W. Gatlin.

deposited during two separate occupations. The trash from the third occupation was lying over that from the second occupation, at least in the center of the midden. They randomly selected twelve 2×2−meter units for excavation and excavated an additional thirty-four square meters to expose two structures found under the trash. Seventy square meters were excavated to uncover human burials. In total, a quarter of the midden (152 square meters of 596) was excavated.

Area III was between the components and surrounded the structural portion of the site. Fourteen percent of Area III was excavated to clarify the relationships among the three components and to test for structures and features that did not show on the surface.

Once the site's surface had been cleared and gridded and the excavation sample had been selected, the archaeologists could start digging. The excavation crew consisted of a site supervisor, four student archaeologists, and sixteen Native Americans divided into two-person excavation crews (Figure 4-8). The site supervisor was responsible for coordinating the excavations: seeing that all structures, features, and randomly selected units were dug and that forms and maps were completed for them. Most of the eight crews excavated inside structures: three on the rubble mounds, and two inside the depressions that probably marked collapsed pit structures. The other three crews were assigned to randomly selected squares in the

Figure 4-8. Each student archaeologist worked with four excavators; the excavators worked in pairs, one digging and one screening. It was the student's job to make sure that they were digging the right unit and that all materials taken from that unit were correctly tagged and inventoried. The archaeologist's most time-consuming responsibility, however, was to write notes describing every facet of the excavations.

Box 4-2. In many ways, the excavation of a site dating to the Puebloan period is more routine than excavations of Archaic or Basketmaker sites. Remains of many Puebloan structures and features are visible, so the excavators can anticipate where walls, floors, and roof-fall will be found. They can also predict the form that the structures will take: masonry rooms have stone walls and earthen or slab floors; jacals have post-lined walls; and pit structures have earthen walls and floors.

In contrast, archaeologists rarely know what they are going to find on earlier sites. Structures occur in almost any form except masonry construction, and both features and structures seem to be scattered at random around the site. Thus, although excavation of a site as large as D:11:2068 presents the logistical problem of keeping many laborers efficiently busy, the site is relatively easy to interpret.

trash middens, where the excavators expected to find most of the artifacts and human burials. The analysis of these artifacts would give them a good idea of how long the site had been occupied and help guide excavations.

In general, site D:11:2068 was a typical Puebloan site, but a few surprises were unearthed (Figure 4-9; Box 4-2). The oldest occupation, in the northern portion, consisted of one masonry structure, an attached **jacal,** and two pit structures. A third pit structure, recorded as Structure 3, was unexpectedly found ninety feet south of the other early structures. It was buried under the trash dumped during the most recent occupation. The excavators had been digging in one of the randomly selected units in the midden. They first suspected that something different was happening when they saw how thick the trash layer was. It was unusual for midden deposits to be more than three feet deep, and they had already dug almost six feet down through typical midden soil containing charcoal, ash, and many broken artifacts. The soil changed color and texture below about three feet, but there was still plenty of charcoal and artifacts.

At first the archaeologists thought they had found a burial pit. They knew that prehistoric people were frequently buried in trash deposits, probably because the midden soil was loose and easy to dig. However, a burial pit is usually less than three feet across; this disturbance was uniform over the entire four-square-meter test unit and was far too large to be a burial

pit. Finally, at six feet below ground surface, the excavators found a hard clay surface. As they dug beyond the original unit, they found the walls of a pithouse (Structure 3). The walls could be distinguished from the soil that had filled the house because they were more firmly packed and contained no artifacts, charcoal, or ash. But the excavators had to dig through the wall into the undisturbed, or culturally sterile, soil to see this difference. Profile drawings showed the sharp distinction between the walls and the fill.

They found a hearth, a bell-shaped storage pit, and several manos on the floor. A tunnel, which extended through the southeastern wall to the ground surface, had vented smoke from the structure. Two clay wall foundations radiating from the hearth partitioned the area east of the hearth from the rest of the structure. A third clay ridge divided this eastern section into two subsections (Figure 4-10). A shallow depression, eight inches across, was immediately northwest of the hearth. It was filled to the rim with sand that could not have blown into the pithouse after it was abandoned, since this sand was found only inside the hole. The excavators thought it possible that the sand-filled hole (Feature 121) was the remains of a **sipapu,** the mythical entrance to the spirit world.

The entire structure was filled with midden deposits, and the whole area was covered with an additional three feet of trash dumped during the third and final occupation. The excavators screened many artifacts from this

Figure 4-9 (left). Structures on Puebloan sites are often found in a predictable arrangement: the masonry rooms face southeast and are flanked by jacals; the kiva, a pit structure used for religious ceremonies, is situated in front of the masonry rooms; and the trash is on the southeastern edge of the site.

Figure 4-10 (right). The floors of early Puebloan pithouses are often subdivided by walls (called wing-walls) radiating out from the firepit. These walls divided the pithouse into distinct areas—possibly for specific activities like food preparation or chipped stone tool production, or possibly to separate "male" areas from "female" areas.

Figure 4-11 (left). Burned beams from the supports or roofs of pithouses were sent to the Laboratory of Tree-Ring Research at the University of Arizona in Tucson to be dated by dendrochronologists. Because they had been burned and buried, beams from collapsed pit structures were especially likely to have been preserved.

Figure 4-12 (right). The extent of sandstone rubble suggested that there had been a large masonry structure, but the archaeologists were confused at the small quantity of rubble. Either the rooms had only a masonry foundation with brush and mud superstructures, or the masonry had been removed and reused by later inhabitants.

upper layer of fill; but because they dated almost two hundred years after Structure 3 was occupied, they provided no information about it. In fact, it was these deposits that so effectively hid all evidence of the pit structure. Structure 3 would not have been found if the archaeologists had excavated only areas where structures were evident on the surface.

Below the trash layer, the excavators reached a layer of sandy soil that had blown into Structure 3 after it had been abandoned and its roof had collapsed. This soil included small particles of windblown charcoal and artifacts that had been washed into the depression by rain and had probably been deposited during or after the first and second occupations of site D:11:2068. They found one burned log above the southeastern wall. If it was part of the materials used in the construction of the pithouse, this beam would be the most likely material for an **independent date** for the structure (Figure 4-11).

The archaeologists suspected the second occupation at site D:11:2068 to be slightly later than the first and to be the largest of the three. It consisted of a large masonry roomblock, subdivided into five rooms; five deep pit structures; one shallow pit structure; two jacals; and a very extensive trash midden. The masonry rooms, one of the deep pithouses, one jacal, and the trash were arranged like a typical Puebloan site. The archaeologists consid-

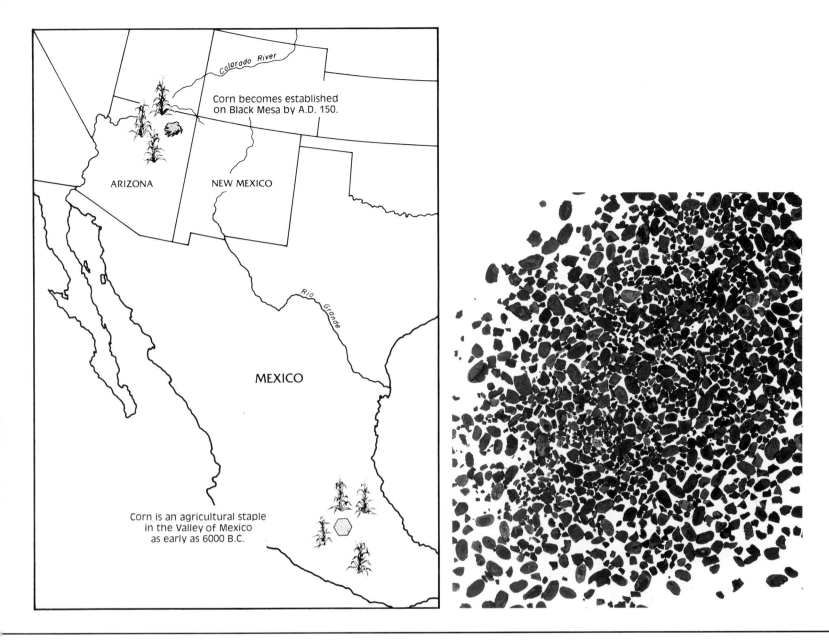

Corn becomes established
on Black Mesa by A.D. 150.

ARIZONA

NEW MEXICO

MEXICO

Corn is an agricultural staple
in the Valley of Mexico
as early as 6000 B.C.

ered the presence and locations of the other structures unusual. Almost all were burned, suggesting that fire destroyed Component II.

Sandstone rubble was spread over a large area but was relatively sparse (Figure 4-12). Excavation showed that the rooms had masonry and slab foundations with wooden and mud **superstructures.** Four of the five rooms had floors lined with slabs, but none had any internal features such as hearths or storage pits. The rooms were all quite small, generally less than eight feet on a side, and their floors were approximately one to two feet below ground surface. Since they were so small, with no internal features and artifacts, the excavators felt that the rooms had been used for storing food and other perishable materials. They certainly would have been cramped and spartan living quarters. This interpretation was supported by the astonishing amount of carbonized corn and beans found in the room.

It was obvious to the excavators that all the rooms had burned, apparently so quickly that there was no time to save the foods stored in them. They found a layer of corn-on-the-cob and loose kernels in all the rooms. They also excavated beans and basketry remains in Structure 5, where the beans had apparently been placed in baskets along with the corn (Figures 4-13, 4-14).

The fire also baked the mud that had been used as **daub** in the rooms'

Figure 4-13 (left). Corn agriculture was not invented in the arid plateaus of the Southwest. Archaeologists found evidence that corn agriculture was practiced in Mexico several thousand years earlier than in the Southwest. Corn was probably first cultivated in the Southwest about 1000 B.C. and caught on widely and quickly after that.

Figure 4-14 (right). Beans are an even rarer find than corn. Prepared by boiling rather than parching, they are even less likely than corn to be accidentally carbonized and preserved. Further, pollen from bean plants is extremely fragile and generally does not fossilize to become part of the pollen record. Finding so many beans was extremely unusual. The beans were so well preserved that their small sprouts were intact, telling the archaeologists that they had burned in midwinter.

Figure 4-15. Among the burials found at site D:11:2068 was that of an older woman. Her body was tightly flexed and placed in a pit excavated into the trash midden. Accompanying her were seven ceramic vessels, including the bird-shaped painted bowl shown on the far right.

superstructures. The excavators found pieces of baked mud that still had impressions from the branches and reeds used to construct the walls. The plant impressions were so well fired that they had survived the thousand years since the fire that had formed them, and they were so clear that the plant specialists could identify the plants that had made them.

Structure 4, the central structure at the second occupation, was a deep pithouse located between the storage rooms and the trash midden. It was very large (twenty-five feet across) and deep (almost six feet below the surface). The floor was subdivided into four sections by **wing-walls** that radiated from the double hearths. Sixty-three posts interspersed with sandstone slabs and clay plaster formed the outer walls. Most of the posts were pinyon and juniper, trees that are well adapted to the arid conditions on Black Mesa and commonly found near site D:11:2068 today. However, the excavators noted that three of the posts were cottonwood, a tree that grows on wet river floodplains. On the floor they found groundstone tools, two complete but broken grayware jars, and three pieces of carved wood. Because of the large size of this pithouse and its central location among the structures of the second component, the archaeologists decided that it was a communal room, used by most or all of the villagers. Structure 4 too was destroyed by the fires that consumed many of the Component II structures.

The excavators found many features both inside and outside the struc-

tures southeast of the roomblock. Most were cooking and heating hearths, storage pits, slab-lined cists (also probably for storage), and structural elements like **ventilator shafts** and slabs; but three were human burials.

Two of the bodies had been interred with little ceremony, but an older woman had been placed in a pit two feet below the trash midden. Her body was flexed, with her knees drawn up under her chin. A metate lay against the left side of her body, and a sandstone slab had been placed over the pit. Seven ceramic vessels, including a seed jar, a pitcher, and a bowl, were arranged on the floor of the pit. The most unusual was a painted bowl made in the form of a bird. It appeared to the archaeologists that this woman was well loved or important enough to warrant this special treatment at death (Figure 4-15).

Only four of the Component II structures, one jacal and three deep pithouses, had not burned. The jacal sheltered a relatively small area (about sixty square feet) into which six storage pits were crowded. The pithouses ranged from one foot to over three feet deep, and each was slightly under fifty square feet in area. Excavators found hearths in three of them and a sand-filled pit in the floor of the fourth. A Kana-a Black-on-white jar was found in one. Because these structures had not burned, few organic remains were preserved, and presumably their inhabitants packed up and took away all items that were still usable when they abandoned the site.

The third occupation consisted of a storage room, a **kiva,** two pithouses, and what appeared to be a jacal. The storage room was constructed from masonry blocks and had a sand floor. A thick layer of charcoal found above the floor was probably the remnants of the structure's burned and collapsed roof. The storage room was built on top of parts of two of the Component II features, but the storage room itself had no features.

The archaeologists thought it interesting that although there was only one masonry room, its rubble mound was the largest of the three. Apparently, builders from each occupation scavenged building materials from earlier abandoned structures. The Component II masonry rooms were probably built from materials from the Component I structures, and the Component III rooms had materials from both Component I and Component II structures. Because there were no Anasazi reoccupations of the ridge after the third component, the structures were allowed to deteriorate in place. All the sandstone used in the Component III masonry room was left and eventually formed the comparatively large rubble mound found by the archaeologists.

The kiva, a ceremonial room, was keyhole-shaped and lined with masonry. Its wall was stepped to form a bench that ringed the interior of the structure. A black-on-white jar had been set in a pit dug into the bench (Figure 4-16). The floor, which was more than six feet below the ground surface, cut into a coal seam.

The two pithouses were less than three feet deep. One was lined with masonry and had twenty-nine support posts (all pinyon and juniper) in its walls. The other had slab and post walls that probably supported a jacal superstructure. Inside each pithouse were a hearth, a storage pit, metates, and manos.

The trash deposited during the third occupation was surprisingly deep, despite the few structures built and used then. The fact that the Component III trash was deeper than the Component II trash suggested to the excavators that although fewer people had inhabited Component III (based on the number of habitation structures), they had lived there longer than any of the older occupations.

ANALYSIS: JUNE–AUGUST 1981

Astonished, the laboratory director looked up from the inventory sheets she was checking. One of the trucks from the new site, site D:11:2068, had returned to camp—and it was only midmorning. Because the sites were so far from camp, often up to fifteen miles away, and because the roads were so poor, the site supervisors were under strict orders not to waste time driving back to camp at midday. The crew should have had all the forms, equipment, food, and water they would need for the day. The lab director and her assistants had helped them pack. Something must be wrong.

Figure 4-16. The ceremonial room, or kiva, built during the third occupation of the site was masonry-lined and keyhole-shaped. A bench ringed the interior of the structure, and there was a black-on-white jar in a pit excavated into the bench.

Figure 4-17 (right). Each pottery type was assigned a name that told the archaeologists something about where it came from and what it looked like. For example, Black Mesa Black-on-white was made in the vicinity of Black Mesa and the vessels were decorated with black paint on a white background.

Figure 4-18 (below). The other analytical system used in the laboratory is based on a limited number of attributes. Certain design elements on painted whiteware pottery are far better temporal indicators than any of the types. Types are defined by combinations of many attributes all occurring together; some are temporally sensitive, some are not. Looking at types has the effect of clouding the precision of those attributes that do vary over time. Another added benefit to attribute analysis is that often only large potsherds can be typed; much smaller potsherds are analytically useful with the attribute system.

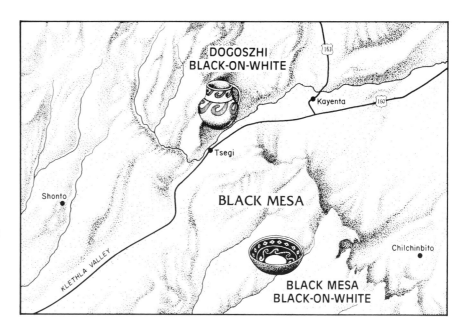

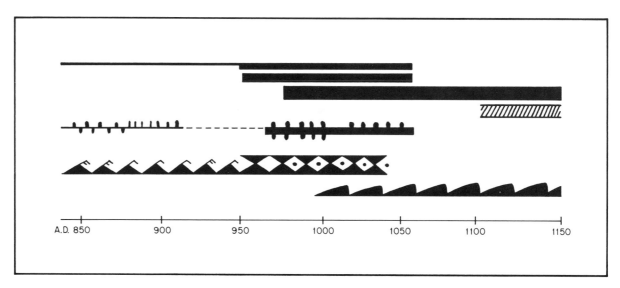

The site supervisor pulled to a stop alongside the entry to the laboratory. There was no problem. The crew had collected so many artifacts from the site's surface that they had already filled the three lidded trash cans used to store artifacts in the field. If they waited until the end of the day, they would have had to truck several loads of artifacts between site D:11:2068 and camp, and the lab assistants would have had to work until well after dinner inventorying everything collected that day. Because both field and lab personnel would have been working while they were tired, mistakes would have been more likely. Bringing the artifacts in early was by far the most efficient procedure. This way they could be inventoried in comparative leisure, and since it was a sunny, windless day, the lab workers could start washing the artifacts.

Each day, once they had checked the information written on each bag or tag against the inventory sheets, the lab assistants sorted the artifacts into groups (ceramic, lithic, and groundstone) and placed them by the laboratory door to be washed.

The artifacts were washed outside. Peabody Coal Company had piped water to the camp, and the workers (all Navajo and Hopi women who lived nearby) filled buckets from a hose in the washing area. Each bag of artifacts was gently emptied into a strainer, and the strainer was dipped into the water. This helped ensure that none of the artifacts would be inadver-

Figure 4-19. A ceramics analyst at work.

tently left in the bottom of the bucket and mixed in with the next bagful. If that happened, the artifact was worse than lost; it would have an incorrect provenience, and perhaps it would even be mixed in with artifacts from a different site and then interpreted in the wrong context.

After the women washed, dried, and rebagged the potsherds, they labeled them and wrote the site number and the bag number on each one. The ceramics analysts then separated the labeled pottery from each bag into **wares** (Figures 4-17, 4-18, 4-19; Boxes 4-3, 4-4). The wares were then subdivided into types, which are good **temporal indicators.** By the end of the field season, their final tally was 121 pieces of San Juan Red Ware; 665 Tsegi Orange Ware; 11,962 Tusayan White Ware; and 25,012 Tusayan Gray Ware—a huge amount of broken pottery (Figures 4-20, 4-21, 4-22). In addition, there were several whole or reconstructable vessels: nine jars, three bowls, three scoops, four miniature jars, and three colanders. The whole vessels had generally been found in burned and collapsed pit structures or accompanying burials. There were also fifty potsherds that had been abraded into a semicircle or U-shape. They had been used to scrape and smooth vessel walls while the clay was still wet (Figure 4-23).

As the site was being excavated, the lithics specialists analyzed all 1,822 pieces of chipped stone found there (Boxes 4-5, 4-6). They interpreted the highly varied tool assemblage to mean that tools were made at the site and

Box 4-4. The ceramic wares most frequently found were Tusayan White Ware and Tusayan Gray Ware. Both were made from locally available clays and were tempered with sand. Almost all the Tusayan Gray Ware types were unpainted, but they were decorated with clay banding around the necks, corrugations over part or all of the vessels, or less frequently with incising or appliqués. Tusayan White Ware types were polished, and most had black designs painted on a white background.

San Juan Red Ware potsherds were less common. As the name suggests, these vessels were made of clay that fired to a reddish orange color. Interestingly, their temper was crushed andesite, a volcanic rock that did not occur naturally in the Black Mesa region. The nearest source of andesite was near the San Juan River, in southeastern Utah or southwestern Colorado.

Tsegi Orange Ware was fairly common. Vessels of this type were also made from clay that fired to a reddish orange color, but they were tempered with sand and crushed potsherds. The ceramic analysts could distinguish Tsegi Orange Ware from San Juan Red Ware only by microscopic examination of their pastes to look at the tempering material. On Black Mesa, the beautiful tricolored vessels found on sites inhabited just before the abandonment of the area about A.D. 1150 were Tsegi Orange Wares.

Figure 4-20. Tusayan Gray Wares. 1, 2, 3, 4, Tusayan Corrugated; 5, Lino Gray; 6, Lino Fugitive Red; 7, Tusayan Corrugated; 8, Lino Fugitive Red; 9, 10, Tusayan Corrugated; 11, Lino Fugitive Red; 12, Kana-a Gray; 13, 14, Tusayan Corrugated; 15, Lino Gray; 16, Tusayan Appliqué; 17, Tusayan Corrugated; 18, Lino Fugitive Red; 19, Tusayan Corrugated; 20, Lino Black-on-gray; 21, 22, Tusayan Corrugated; 23, Kana-a Gray; 24, Tusayan Corrugated; 25, 26, Lino Gray; 27, Lino Fugitive Red; 28, Tusayan Corrugated; 29, Lino Fugitive Red; 30, Tusayan Corrugated; 31, Lino Fugitive Red.

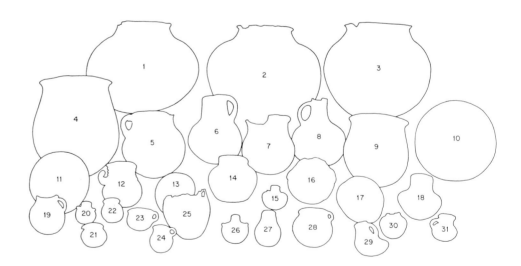

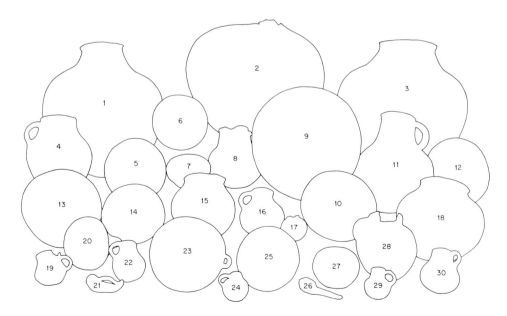

Figure 4-21. Tusayan White Wares. *1, 2, 3, Sosi Black-on-white; 4, Wepo Black-on-white; 5, 6, 7, Black Mesa Black-on-white; 8, Wepo Black-on-white; 9, Flagstaff Black-on-white; 10, 11, Kana-a Black-on-white; 12, Dogoszhi Black-on-white; 13, unidentified; 14, Black Mesa Black-on-white; 15, Dogoszhi Black-on-white; 16, Black Mesa Black-on-white; 17, unidentified; 18, Sosi Black-on-white; 19, unidentified; 20, Black Mesa Black-on-white; 21, unidentified; 22, Kana-a Black-on-white; 23, 24, Black Mesa Black-on-white; 25, 26, unidentified; 27, Kana-a Black-on-white; 28, Black Mesa Black-on-white; 29, unidentified; 30, Black Mesa Black-on-white.*

Figure 4-22. Tsegi Orange Wares and San Juan Red Wares. 1, Tusayan Black-on-red; 2, Medicine Black-on-red; 3, 4, Tusayan Black-on-red; 5, Deadmans Black-on-red; 6, Tusayan Black-on-red; 7, 8, Deadmans Black-on-red; 9, La Plata Black-on-red; 10, Medicine Black-on-red; 11, Tusayan Black-on-red; 12, Deadmans Black-on-red; 13, Bluff Black-on-red; 14, Abajo Red-on-orange; 15, Bluff Black-on-red; 16, Citadel Polychrome; 17, 18, 19, Deadmans Black-on-red; 20, 21, Tusayan Black-on-red; 22, Bluff Black-on-red; 23, Abajo Red-on-orange; 24, Tusayan Black-on-red; 25, Deadmans Black-on-red; 26, Tusayan Black-on-red; 27, Deadmans Black-on-red.

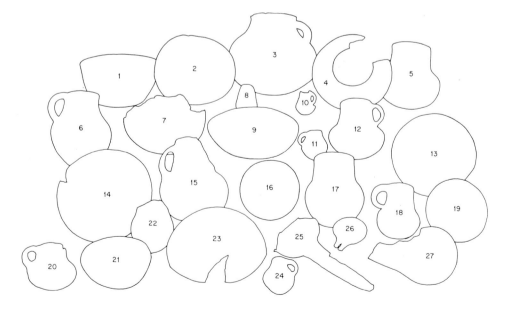

Figure 4-23. Broken pottery was sometimes abraded into semicircular or U-shaped pieces and then used in manufacturing pottery.

that many activities requiring chipped stone took place there. Waste flakes, blanks (roughly shaped but unfinished tools), and finished bifaces, all made from the same raw materials, supported the interpretation. By examining the damage on the edges of tools, the analysts could tell whether those tools were used for planing, scraping, cutting and sawing, chopping, or drilling. Deliberate abrasion on many of the formal tools, such as drills or projectile points, indicated to the analysts that they had been reshaped or resharpened. The fact that they were made of stone that came from many different places suggested that their users were probably trading with other groups.

The lithics analysts also looked at 289 pieces of groundstone. Two of the pithouses on site D:11:2068 held unusually large amounts of groundstone. Four manos, each small enough to be held in one hand, were found on the floor of Structure 3, the isolated pithouse from the first occupation found under later trash deposits. There were ten pieces of groundstone on the floor of the large, centrally located pithouse from the second occupation. These artifacts and the two grayware jars suggested to the archaeologists that the structure burned while it was still being used. Otherwise the groundstone and jars would have been removed and used again elsewhere.

During excavation, the field archaeologists took specimens from each piece of wood used in room construction. The samples were identified by

Figure 4-24. Tree-ring scientists can determine whether a piece of wood has its final growth ring. There may be bark present, or the tunnels of gallery beetles (which live between the bark and the outer edge of the growing tree) may be observable. However, many samples lack an undetermined number of outer rings, perhaps because the piece of wood was shaped for a specific purpose. Tree-ring dates are reported with an indicator of the tree-ring specialists' confidence that the outer ring observed was actually the final growth ring. Unfortunately, few dated specimens have the final ring.
Photograph courtesy of the Laboratory of Tree-Ring Research, University of Arizona.

Box 4-7. A tree ceases growing and producing rings when it dies; thus the final ring dates the death of the tree. However, certain circumstances may make the actual death date difficult to determine, leading to erroneous conclusions about when structures or features were built.

For one thing, some fine adjustments might have been made during construction. A piece of wood is rarely exactly the right size for its intended use, and the builders might have planed a beam to make it fit. Since planing would remove an unknown number of outer growth rings, the ring sequence might yield a date many years earlier than the actual death of the tree. Often growth rings are so narrow that removing the outer inch or so affects the date by a hundred or more years.

Another problem derives from the scarcity of good structural wood in an arid environment like that of Black Mesa. If a structure had deteriorated past repair and a replacement structure was being built, the construction crew might find it easier to reuse major and secondary beams from the abandoned structure than to cut all new wood. Where this has happened, a date based on an old beam used in the new structure would be erroneously early for that structure.

the plant specialist, and the field archaeologists used the information to collect promising samples for tree-ring dating. Most of the wood used to build the structure was pinyon and juniper, but other wood was occasionally found. Several dates were determined on the tree-ring specimens sent to the University of Arizona for analysis. Although there were some problems in interpreting the dates, they generally supported the division of site D:11:2068 into three components (Figure 4-24; Box 4-7).

After the excavations ended, the human skeletal remains from the three burials were shipped to the University of Massachusetts—Amherst for analysis. There **osteologists** examined them carefully and compared the bones with "normal" healthy specimens. This told them many things about who the people were and how they had lived. The three were all adults: two women (one in her early twenties and one forty-one to forty-four years old at death) and one man (forty-four to forty-nine years old). All three had slight flattening at the backs of their skulls caused by being strapped to cradle boards when they were infants.

All three had several dental caries (cavities), suggesting a diet relatively high in starches. The younger woman had a broken nose that had healed before she died, and both the man and the older woman had arthritis. All had evidence of early growth disruptions on their teeth (**enamel hypoplasias**) and on their arm and leg bones (**growth arrest lines**) that sug-

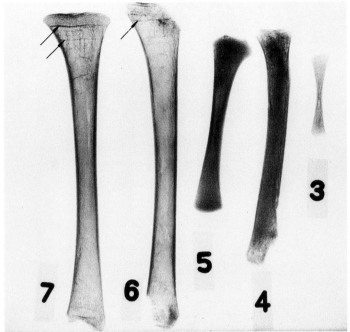

gested chronic health problems between the ages of two and a half and four and a half. According to the osteologists, these problems were probably caused by nutritional stresses during weaning (Figures 4-25, 4-26).

All these different types of laboratory analyses told the archaeologists many things about the occupation of site D:11:2068. However, many questions about the site could not be answered. For one thing, it was not clear whether the site's three occupations were separated in time or were continuous. The first and second occupations were probably quite close in time, perhaps even continuous. But the final occupation most likely occurred a hundred or so years after the second occupation.

Several structures were built during each occupation, but were all built at one time or were some built and used to replace others that had deteriorated? Some of the structures might have been used only seasonally. Pithouses, for example, would have been cramped and dark but comfortably warm in the winter, while more open surface structures like jacals might have been preferred during the summer. Some of the structures, the masonry stone rooms and the centrally located ceremonial pithouses, probably were used communally and were not habitations.

Because the archaeologists did not know when each structure had been built or how the structures had been used, they could not tell exactly how many people had lived at the site. The large number of structures from the

Figure 4-25 (left). *Enamel hypoplasias, or lines on teeth where no enamel was formed, indicate major disruptions in the development of children and the age when they occurred. The frequency of enamel hypoplasias between ages two and four suggests that Black Mesa children underwent severe nutritional stress when they were weaned and started on solid diets.*

Figure 4-26 (right). *Disruption in growth, caused by dietary stress among other things, results in areas of densely packed bone cells that show up on X-rays as lines perpendicular to the long axes of the bones. These are growth arrest lines, or Harris lines, and several are indicated on this photograph with arrows.*

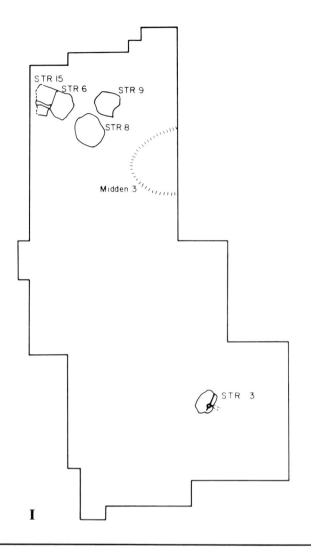

STR 15
STR 6
STR 9
STR 8

Midden 3

STR 3

I

second occupation suggested that many people lived there then, but why should so many people generate so little trash? And why did the occupants of Component III, who built only four structures, produce far more trash than the Component II occupants? The best guess is that many people lived at the site during Component II but only for a short time, and that comparatively few Component III people lived there for a long time (Figure 4-27).

The archaeologists were able to determine that many activities requiring many different kinds of tools and structures took place at site D:11:2068 during all three occupations. The corn and beans found in large numbers suggested the importance of cultivated crops. The reoccupations of the ridge and the presence of the Begays' cornfields in the Moenkopi floodplain attest to the desirability of the location for human settlement and farming. Archaeologists will be working for many years with the remains collected from the site, trying to resolve some of the unanswered questions about the people who once lived there.

WINTER, A.D. 872–873

Too many people had lived here too long. Part of the main village was in ruins: the roof of its communal pithouse had collapsed, and the storage cists behind it were dilapidated. The depression from the collapsed pithouse

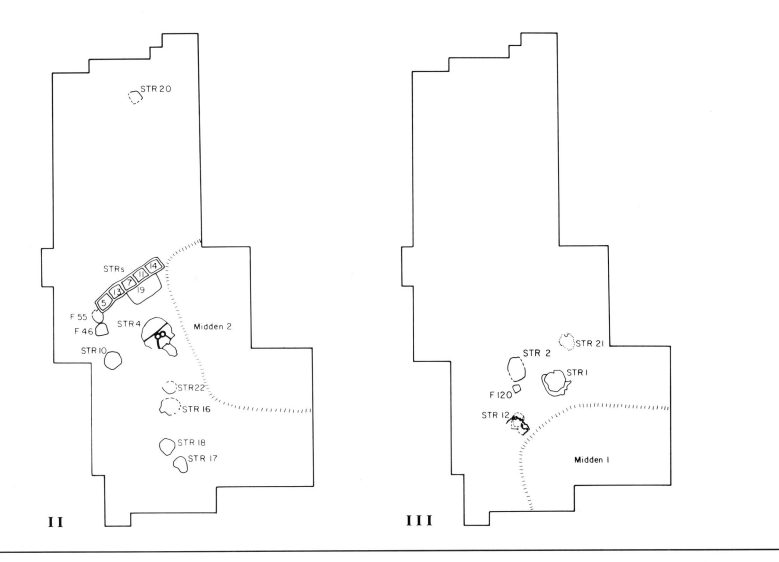

II

III

was being used as a trash dump, and stones from the cists were being re-used at the village and at the two smaller *rancherías* nearby.

Ten families, all related, lived in the three settlements: five at the village and five others at two smaller settlements. The people eked out a living by farming, collecting wild plants, and hunting. Everyone helped with the farming, which occupied almost all their time during the growing season. Women and older children collected seeds, nuts, berries, and plant greens as they became available; men and older boys hunted game.

In the past they had lived comfortably here. There were broad flood-plains for fields and open upland areas that had attracted deer and ante-lope. But the fields had been planted year after year with too little fallow time for soil regeneration, so crop yields had declined. Large game now seemed to avoid the area surrounding their settlements, and the hunters had to go farther and farther to find prey. Wood collecting for fires and con-struction materials had totally used up the dead wood nearby, and people had started cutting live wood for fuel. This would eventually deplete wood and other forest products such as pinyon nuts, juniper berries, and bark. The trees grew so slowly that it would take several human lifetimes to re-generate the forest. Something had to be done.

People on hunting or collecting forays had noticed a suitable place for a village two or three miles upstream. The floodplain offered a beautiful cottonwood grove and several potential fields, and the woodland grew right

Figure 4-27. Even though there were many structures at D:11:2068, they were not all built and used at the same time. Analysis of the artifacts excavated from the site indicated that Components I and II had been oc-cupied during the A.D. 800s and that Component III had been occupied during the 1100s.

Figure 4-28. After the fields had been cleared and planted, the pioneers excavated the walls and floor of the communal pithouse.

to the edge of the ridge that backed the site. Two families, consisting of two sisters, their husbands, and five children, were eager to move. The grandmother did not wish to be parted from her daughters and grandchildren, so she and her mate decided to move as well.

Since success at this endeavor was to everyone's advantage, those who preferred to remain were supportive and freely offered food, equipment, and labor. If the pioneers prospered, their absence would ease the economic burden at the old site, and they would be excellent trading partners to their friends and relatives who remained.

They would move as soon as the spring planting could begin. The men and older boys would go first to start clearing the fields and stockpiling construction materials. The others would follow after a week or so, accompanied by a work party from their old home. Together they would plant the fields on the floodplain and excavate the walls and floor of the communal pithouse at the new site (Figure 4-28).

SPRING, A.D. 873

The families had selected well when they chose this place for their new home. True, it was only a couple of miles upstream from their old home, but it was less crowded. Their new settlement had all the advantages of the old one and more. There were expanses of floodplain, enough land to let spent fields lie fallow and regenerate. There were also flat upland areas for dry fields. With both types of fields planted, some crops would mature regardless of the rainfall; the upland fields would do well in a year so wet that the floodplain fields were washed away, and in dry years the floodplain fields would flourish while the upland crops withered and died. It took time and much planning to plant all the fields, but the settlers knew it ensured their survival. Although they still collected wild seeds, pinyon nuts, and juniper berries, they could not rely on these noncultivated foods to feed everyone.

Small game would be abundant here, as it had been at their old home, because trash and the planted fields attracted small rodents, especially rabbits, which the boys and girls could kill while they helped tend the fields. But this new spot also had plentiful large game like deer, mountain sheep, and antelope, and there were no neighbors to compete for it.

Their new home was also very close to the pinyon and juniper forest and its many resources. The game animals were there, and there would be pinyon nuts and juniper berries to harvest. Pinyon trees were notoriously erratic in producing nuts, but a good year's harvest would provide a storable

Figure 4-29. The pinyon trees produced nuts erratically—once every seven years was the average. The trees had to be watched carefully, first to determine whether nuts would be produced, and second to ensure that the people were able to harvest the nuts before birds and rodents ate them.

and tasty source of fatty protein for many months. The only problem, a big one, was that the trees produced abundant nuts so infrequently—only about once every seven years (Figure 4-29).

The forest also provided them with wood. Pinyon grew straight, and after its sticky sap dried, the settlers could use it for construction. They would also use juniper as a building material, with the added bonus that it would repel insects with its strong scent. Unfortunately, it curved and twisted as it grew, and it was difficult to find pieces long enough for primary supports. But juniper could be used for smaller elements, and the shredded bark had many uses including kindling, roofing, and diapers. Deadfall from both kinds of trees would provide firewood for cooking and heating.

They had heard stories of an earlier settlement here, and they were finding some indications that the stories were true. A generation ago there had been so few people in the region that villagers would just move whenever the surrounding area was overhunted or overcollected. Once established, a settlement might be periodically abandoned as some or all of its occupants moved to hunt, collect plants, or cultivate plants in other places. By the looks of it, the earlier occupants had cultivated fields for a few years, hoping for surplus production to tide them over in lean periods. The little garbage they had left behind was no longer smelly or attracting rodent pests, and

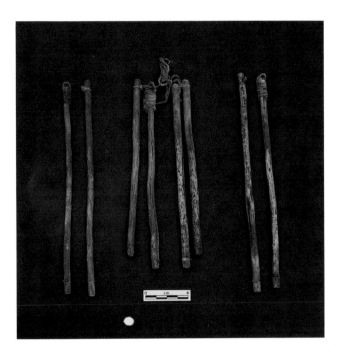

the new inhabitants reused some of the old building stone and wood in new structures.

The first job for the new settlers was to open new fields. Unless they had sufficient food, they would not make it through the winter. They cleared sage from the floodplain and planted seed corn deeply in small hillocks of soil. Deep planting protected the germinating plants from late frosts and from the May and June winds. They planted beans in the same hillocks as the corn, so that the bean vines could climb the cornstalks as both plants grew.

While the fields were being planted, the children, under the guidance of their grandmother, gathered the smaller pieces of wood and juniper bark that were to be used for construction, firewood, and roofing. Then the young adults finished the communal pithouse and began to build their summer jacal and a storage room for anticipated crop surpluses and other winter provisions. When they had completed these buildings, their most basic needs were satisfied: everyone had shelter, even though it was a bit crowded. Other houses could be built as time permitted.

The people now settled into a more routine daily schedule. The children went to the fields each day to protect the growing plants from birds and rodents. The young boys practiced their hunting skills on the rabbits that

Figure 4-30. The Puebloans and Basketmakers hunted rabbits and other small game with sticks or with snare traps. These remarkably preserved snare traps are almost two thousand years old. They were found at Three Fir Shelter, a Basketmaker II cave on the north rim of Black Mesa.

Figure 4-31. Each woman prepared the daily food for her family, using her metate and mano to grind corn and other seeds into flour.

infested the fields. The ones they killed were a tasty and consistent protein source for the whole group (Figure 4-30).

The women, tending the very young children as they worked, spent most of their day preparing food. Although the older children helped collect firewood, more was always needed, and sometimes the women lent a hand. Each woman prepared food for her family daily. Grinding seeds, especially corn, into flour was the most time-consuming task; hours were spent every day at the metate and mano (Figure 4-31). The flour was cooked into gruel and baked into a thin, paper-like bread. When available, greens and meat complemented the diet. The meat was usually rabbit, but occasionally deer, antelope, or mountain sheep provided a special treat.

Clay and **temper** for pottery were easy to find; they were collected in the fall and prepared and formed into vessels during the confining winter months. After a long, slow drying period, the vessels were fired on windless spring days. Although any of the women could form some kind of vessel from the pliable clay, very few were skillful.

The most skillful of all was the grandmother, who made excellent neck-banded cooking jars and pitchers. Mixing the clay and temper in the right proportions and shaping a vessel that would withstand heat from a direct fire was an art. Her skills were valuable to the group both directly and indirectly: they always had fine cookware, and her pottery was exchanged for

commodities and produce from other groups (Figure 4-32). Even people far distant from them were eager for the chance to trade for the jars she made.

Crop failures were experienced by everyone, but they were rarely widespread. So even if food was in short supply at one village, another might have more than enough. Valuable commodities like the cookware could be "banked" and traded for food when necessary, or occasional food surpluses could be traded for the special crafts of other groups. The jar used to store their seed corn was one such item. They had traded for this beautiful bird effigy years ago, after an especially good growing year had produced exceptional yields. It had been cherished ever since and had been with the group for several generations.

During the growing season, especially during planting and harvesting, the men were busy tending the fields. Different fields were planted at different times with hopes that all would mature. However, the length of the growing season was variable, and late spring frosts or early winter freezes often killed plants that germinated too early or matured too late. Some plants usually matured, and occasionally all of them did, providing a welcome surplus.

After the harvest, the men had time to repair damaged farming and hunting tools and to make new ones. One man made the small points that tipped their arrows, but most of their "tools" were simply sharp flakes

Figure 4-32. Shaping clay into neck-banded cooking jars was both an art and a science. The jars could be banked and traded for produce in case of crop failures.

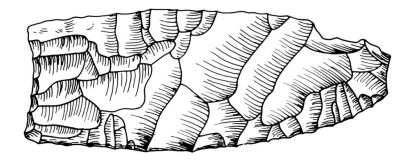

Figure 4-33. The Puebloans were as fascinated with the beautiful points made long ago as we are today. This spear point was found near Kayenta, Arizona, and is probably ten thousand years old.

struck from a stone core. Efficient use of the core to get the most usable flakes possible was considered more important than skillful tool-making. Occasionally someone would find a long thin projectile of red or white stone, and the whole group marveled at its size and beauty. No one made points like those now; they were far too large for arrows (Figure 4-33).

Most of the stone they used to make tools came from trading partners who lived twenty miles to the northeast. They quarried purple chert from a source near Owl Rock in the red rock country (Figure 4-34). The Owl Rock people also had smaller amounts of stone obtained from their other trading partners, as did the Black Mesa people. The Black Mesans did not have direct access to many sources of chippable stone; they obtained most of their stone in exchange for crop surpluses, pinyon nuts, or neck-banded jars—whatever happened to be available and in demand in a given year.

Household maintenance required constant attention. The masonry storerooms were the least used; since large quantities of surplus food and infrequently used ritual paraphernalia were stored there, there was little day-to-day use that would cause deterioration. However, the mud and daub jacals needed repair after every major rainstorm and after the winter thaws. New mud was mixed and applied to areas of the walls or roofs where the old had sloughed off. Pithouse walls were underground, but their roofs were level with the settlement's courtyard, and foot traffic caused them to deteriorate.

Figure 4-34. The monolith that we call Owl Rock marks the location of a large chert source that may have been quarried by Black Mesa's Puebloans. Black Mesa lies about ten miles south of Owl Rock and forms the horizon in this photograph.

Large, thin sandstone slabs were placed around the perimeter of the pithouse roofs to warn people away, but accidents happened, especially among the children, who often became so engrossed in their games that they forgot and stumbled past the slabs onto the roofs.

Additional structures were built as time permitted. If the harvests were good, they would need more storerooms, and ideally there would be a pithouse for each family to live in during the winter months. The pithouses were dark, stuffy, and crowded, but they were also warm. Except for the jacal, they used the structures less frequently during the summer; many of them camped overnight in the fields, and those who stayed at home usually slept outside during the warm weather. On warm days everyone worked outside, keeping gnats and other biting insects at bay with smoke from smudge fires.

A wall was built around the main part of the site to screen off the trash midden as it grew and became unsightly and smelly. The prevailing wind was from the southwest, so placement of the trash to the east of and downhill from the structures did a great deal to keep it from becoming too much of a nuisance. But rodents were attracted to the garbage and feces in the trash, and snakes—including rattlesnakes—were attracted to the rodents. The wall protected the homes from rodent and reptile pests and reminded people to dump their trash away from the living space.

WINTER, A.D. 876–877

Each family now had its own winter home, a small pithouse, but family members slept there only during the cold winter months. These pithouses were too cramped for socializing, so the communal pithouse was used as a gathering place. During the late spring months the men had used it when making preparations to greet the **Kachinas** upon their return from their winter home in the mountains far to the southwest (Figure 4-35). The communal pithouse was so heavily used that it had been necessary to make roof repairs just last fall, and while the men were repairing it, they had noticed how dry the timbers and thatch had become.

This winter was particularly severe, with constant cold and stormy weather. The people were grateful that the previous years had been bountiful and that there was surplus food in the storerooms, but the cold weather and forced inactivity was hard on everyone, especially the children and their grandmother. They all doubted that the grandmother would survive the winter. There was nothing specifically wrong, but she was forty-three years old and had lived a long and hard life. She was so stiff and in such pain that she could no longer help in the fields or go on long foraging trips; worse, her fingers had lost their dexterity, and she could no longer make cooking

jars. She knew she had outlived her usefulness and that she was a burden to the group.

The days began to lengthen; cold westerly storms were less frequent and the intervening clear days were warm. The snow was melting, seeping into the soil, promising a good growing year for the pinyon and juniper trees as well as ideal early growing conditions for the community's crops. Stored food would tide the people over the rest of the lean period until the early wild plants started growing. There might even be food left over to provide a buffer should the coming summer growing season not fulfill its promise.

Although the days were warmer, the nights were frigid. The grandmother, her mate, and one of their daughters, who was still healing from injuries suffered in a fall last autumn, continued to sleep in the communal pithouse. This shelter was spacious, and the three could stretch out and sleep in luxurious warmth and comfort.

When it was over, the survivors agreed that they had noticed a brightening late that night—even from inside their pit homes. When someone finally investigated, it was too late to do anything. Apparently the heating fire in the communal pithouse had not been properly banked, and a spark had ignited the tinder-dry roof. The fire had already spread to the jacal and was threatening the storerooms when it was discovered.

Figure 4-35. Kachinas are supernatural beings who bring rain and other good things to the Puebloans. They are often represented as wood carvings or as decorative motifs on pottery. Hopi jar and Kachina from the collections of the Museum of Northern Arizona, Flagstaff.

There was virtually nothing to fight the fire with. Drinking water for each family's use was stored in jars, but it amounted to only about ten gallons. People could only toss sand on the flames and hope for the best, while some of the boys made repeated trips through the small storeroom doors to salvage food.

The fire burned itself out within an hour. It had charred the roof of the communal pithouse, cutting off escape for the three people inside and suffocating them. From there it had spread to the jacal and burned it to the ground. The storeroom roofs were the last to go, along with such of the rooms' contents as had not been retrieved by the boys. They had enough food for the rest of the winter if they were careful, and their homes were intact. The rest of the winter and early spring would be spent in some discomfort, but they would probably survive.

The funerals were held the next day. Three graves were dug into the soft dirt and debris of the trash dump (Figure 4-36). The soil beneath the trash was unfrozen, and the pits were enlarged to accommodate the tightly flexed bodies. The grandmother was buried with her bird effigy seed jar. The survivors were devastated by her death, even though they had all known that she would probably not survive the winter. The way she and the others died reminded the survivors of their own mortality; the same thing could happen to any of them. Favorite ceramic vessels were placed in

the burial pit with her as symbols of love and respect. The other two were interred with little ceremony. It was not that they were not cared for, but the unexpected deaths and the destruction of much of their village had overwhelmed the survivors.

The remaining settlers were undecided about what to do come summer. A few wanted to stay and rebuild, but the others took the disaster as an omen and began to speculate about the ruins of the earlier village. What had caused those people to leave? Perhaps there was something unfriendly here that discouraged settlement.

They knew that they could always return to their old home, if only for a few seasons, before renewing their pioneering efforts. They were all related by blood or by marriage to the inhabitants of their old home, and they had given them some surplus food each year. With more food to eat and fewer people to eat it, the old village had enjoyed prosperous times since the move. In a sense, it owed the emigrants a favor, and it appeared that they would now return to collect it.

FALL, A.D. 1120

The farmer stood in his field and surveyed the view up and down the wash channel. There were small villages wherever a minor wash drained

Figure 4-36. The graves were prepared in the soft soil of the trash midden. Ceramic vessels, including the bird effigy jar, were placed with the grandmother.

into the Moenkopi; he could see his own home and one other, and he knew that there were several more upstream as well as downstream from where he was working. Over half of the Moenkopi's floodplain was planted with crops this year, far more than should be under cultivation if the soil were to regenerate itself. The fields required three to seven years' fallow for every year's planting to renew their fertility, but they were getting only one year. Yields had been declining steadily for as long as he could remember.

Some of his relatives had tried to solve the problem of declining fertility and yields by moving upstream from the major washes into smaller and smaller drainages. They could move further upstream because a series of exceptionally wet years provided enough water for crops to germinate and mature. Their initial yields in the upland fields were good; however, as more people followed their initiative, overcrowding caused the same problems of shorter fallow periods, decreasing soil fertility, and declining crop yields. And they had an additional problem: because the upland fields were near the sources of the stream systems, little water flowed along the stream channel to water their fields. When rainfall was heavy, this caused no problems; but when rainfall was light, the crops suffered, and years of light rainfall seemed to be more and more frequent. Downstream fields did not fare as poorly, since they had the benefit of water flowing from a much larger area.

The upstream people had the advantage of being surrounded by the pin-

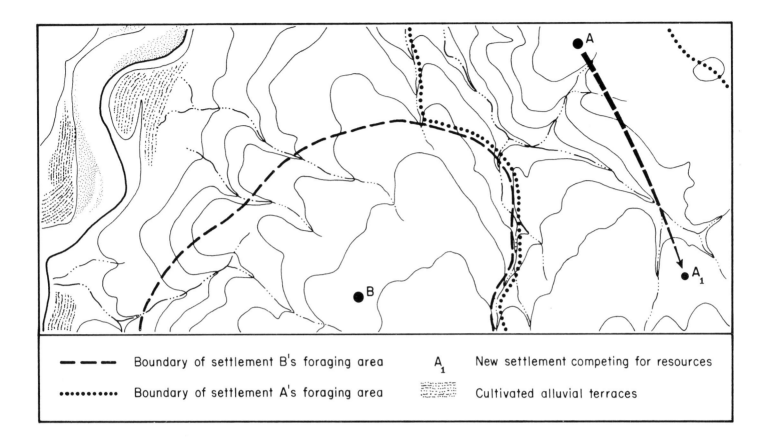

— — —	Boundary of settlement B's foraging area
••••••••••	Boundary of settlement A's foraging area

A₁	New settlement competing for resources
	Cultivated alluvial terraces

yon and juniper forests. They were able to collect wood, pinyon nuts, and juniper bark and berries much more easily than the downstream people. However, this practice had become a source of contention. In years past, the downstream villagers had collected forest products from as far afield as necessary. In years when harvests were poor or nonexistent, they compensated by collecting large quantities of grass seeds, nuts, and berries. If need be, they collected from areas far distant from their villages, near where the upstream settlements were now located. Nowadays, however, someone always seemed to live near the good collecting areas, and these people would already have gathered any wild plant foods that might be available.

This meant that all the people on the northern part of Black Mesa had little in the way of a buffer in the event that their crops fared poorly or failed. And the crops failed more often as soil fertility declined and summers produced less and less rainfall. In the old days, when they were able to collect and hunt in large areas, there was always some source of food that they could fall back on. Moreover, they could often rely on surpluses stored for use during bad times. And when all else failed, they could ask for help from relatives or trading partners, since poor conditions rarely extended over the entire mesa. Now none of their buffers worked. Collecting areas were restricted, and the soil was so poor that surpluses were a thing of the past (Figure 4-37).

Figure 4-37. The movement of people into upland zones had increased the amount of land tilled and planted for fields. However, increased population density had reduced the area that any single family could expect to exploit for wild plants and nuts. In this schematic, the occupants of settlement A₁ are going to have to compete for resources and territory with the occupants of settlements A and B.

Figure 4-38. Infant mortality, often because of weanling diarrhea, was very high. Food shortages and dietary deficiencies were especially hard on young children and on mothers who were breast-feeding their babies. These remains of a newborn were found on another Black Mesa Puebloan site.

The man was sure that the crops maturing in his field would not provide sufficient food for his family during the coming winter. His wife was pregnant again after miscarrying last spring. If this new baby were born, it would enter this world during the hunger months of mid-spring, and there was little chance that it would survive until it was old enough to eat and digest cornmeal gruel; perhaps it would be best if this baby too died before it was fully formed and they had grown to love it (Figure 4-38).

Their older children, both boys, were a great help with all the chores. They collected firewood and helped forage for the few wild plants that grew near their settlement. Both helped in the fields, and the elder was especially good at snaring rabbits—ridding the fields of the pests and supplying some meat for their stew. Soon he would be old enough and sufficiently skilled to accompany his father and the older men on big game hunts. But the hunters rarely caught enough animals to make the hunt worthwhile.

As the man mulled over these problems, he thought of the irony of having an excess of labor but not enough good land to till. He, his wife, and their sons were idle for much of the growing season. Then, in the autumn, their crops matured and the wild plants ripened at the same time; suddenly there was never enough time to accomplish everything that needed to be done. If only there were some way to increase crop yields or to even out the workload.

He was acquainted with the strange farming practices of the people who lived in the long valley just north of the mesa. They planted crops in the strangest place: around the bases of sand dunes. They claimed that rainwater drained through the dune while the sand kept it from evaporating. Eventually the water reached the edge of the dune, where it fed the crops. It must be working, since he had seen plants growing there.

Even stranger were stories that these people carried water to their crops. That just wasn't natural; and yet, if the Black Mesa farmer could somehow use extra labor in that way to increase his yields, it just might be the solution to his problems. He could not imagine how to water his fields. The stream channel was steep and the floodplain narrow, and there was no place to divert the water on the few occasions when it was available. The washes, when they flowed, were raging torrents. It was hard to imagine getting the water to the plants any way other than carrying it jar by jar, and that would never work. Perhaps there was a better way in the valley.

He would have to visit his friends and relatives in the valley this winter anyway. His family would have to trade some of their durable goods, perhaps the beautiful black and white olla, for food. Maybe if valley farming methods were so demanding of labor and so productive, there would be a place for a hardworking family like his. There just didn't seem to be much point in remaining on the mesa. Maybe they should move to the valley.

LATE PUEBLOAN AND HISTORIC

CHAPTER 5

Archaeologists have found virtually no evidence that people lived on northern Black Mesa between A.D. 1150 and 1800. The latest tree-ring date from a prehistoric site is A.D. 1141, and since it is likely that the Anasazi continued to live there for some time after that structure was built, the site was abandoned at about A.D. 1150. This does not mean that no one ever visited northern Black Mesa after A.D. 1150. On the contrary, over the years many people probably traveled to the area to hunt, to cut wood, and to collect pinyon nuts and other plant foods. But they apparently stayed only a short while, leaving little behind that could be identified and dated by archaeologists working hundreds of years later.

One radiocarbon sample dated to A.D. 1281. The burned wood was collected from a hearth that was excavated in the fill of a pithouse approximately five feet above the floor. Ceramics from the rest of the site were made at approximately A.D. 1000, so the site had been abandoned for almost three hundred years when it was reoccupied. The final occupants, the makers of the hearth, were probably hunting or collecting plants and sought shelter from a storm or for the night. The pithouse on the abandoned site was only partly filled with sand at the time, and the shallow depression provided protection from the wind and a soft cushion on which the hunters could rest. They built a fire but did not stay long enough to break or discard any artifacts.

Figure 5-1. Kiet Siel ruin, in Navajo National Monument, was built about one hundred years after what became the Peabody lease area was abandoned by the Anasazi.

This kind of occupation was probably typical of how northern Black Mesa was used after A.D. 1150. Few artifacts, usually stone chips or broken arrow points, were left behind, and they were scattered almost at random over the landscape. Such artifacts would be difficult to distinguish from the massive amount of debris left by the many Puebloans who had lived on northern Black Mesa between A.D. 825 and 1150.

The later visitors probably left the remains of hearths, as did the earlier Puebloans, Basketmakers, and Archaic peoples. However, if they discarded no **diagnostic** artifacts—artifacts that tell archaeologists something about who left them and when they were left—these hearths would look just like earlier ones. They could be radiocarbon-dated, but this technique is very expensive, and it is unlikely that archaeologists would spend thousands of dollars analyzing charcoal from all the hearths scattered throughout the area. In general, archaeologists realize that they are unlikely ever to find traces of some activities.

The Puebloan peoples who abandoned their northern Black Mesa homes at A.D. 1150 probably moved south. Although there were people living just north of Black Mesa at the time, in Tsegi Canyon, Long House Valley, and Klethla Valley, there are no signs that an immigrant group joined the valley peoples. The little archaeological work that has been conducted south of the lease area shows that people were living there as well after the lease

area was abandoned; unfortunately, survey coverage is too sparse to tell the archaeologists whether that is where the northern Black Mesans moved.

After the people left northern Black Mesa, they tried new ways of eking out a living from the harsh environment. They lived in larger villages, farmed with new techniques, and experimented with different styles of arts and crafts. By A.D. 1250, they had settled into a handful of much larger communities in southern and central Black Mesa and in the maze of canyons and valleys to the north. The one thing the site locations had in common was the fact that they were located near springs or small streams.

There were more people, and they clustered near increasingly scarce sources of water. Thus their communities were much larger than earlier ones. Furthermore, there is evidence at most of these sites for water conservation methods like impoundment dams for domestic water. A number of these later Puebloan sites were situated under huge rock overhangs in narrow canyons: the famous and picturesque cliff dwellings, such as Betatakin and Kiet Siel, which are major tourist attractions today (Figure 5-1).

Puebloan society had undergone many major social changes: there were much larger agglomerations of population than in earlier times; the individual dwellings were more communal; and there were large community construction efforts, such as dams. But these did not last long, for by A.D. 1300 environmental conditions worsened and even the canyons and valleys

north of Black Mesa were abandoned. The entire population of north-eastern Arizona was concentrated along the southern edge of Black Mesa. Despite its hostile appearance, the mesa's southern perimeter provided one essential ingredient for human habitation: a dependable source of water. Many springs occur along the cliffs that make up the southern escarpment of Black Mesa, and people were drawn to this water for domestic use and for irrigation. Puebloan peoples, now called Hopis, still live along the southern edge of Black Mesa (Figures 5-2 and 5-3; Box 5-1).

The first indications of people reusing northern Black Mesa on a comparatively permanent basis come from tree-ring samples dated to the early 1800s. Samples taken from sites on the central and southern portions of the mesa indicate that those areas were reoccupied by the mid-1700s, but north of Black Mesa the remains are no older than the early 1800s. So people apparently moved into the area from the south, then colonized northern Black Mesa, and later moved into the valleys north of the mesa. The wood samples were collected from small, circular structures called forked-stick hogans. Hogans are the typical homes of the Navajo people, and the presence of these structures documents the movement of the Navajos from New Mexico into Arizona.

The Navajo language, one of the Athabaskan group, is closely related to languages spoken by Native Americans who live in the interior of Alaska

Figure 5-2 (*far left*). *The springs that flow at the southern edge of Black Mesa attracted prehistoric immigrants during the late A.D. 1200s. These same springs are used today by the Hopi to irrigate small terrace fields. The fields shown here are located below the modern Hopi village of Hotevilla.*

Figure 5-3 (*above*). *Hopi clan symbols carved on a boulder at Willow Springs, Arizona.*
Copyright 1977 by Karl Kernberger.

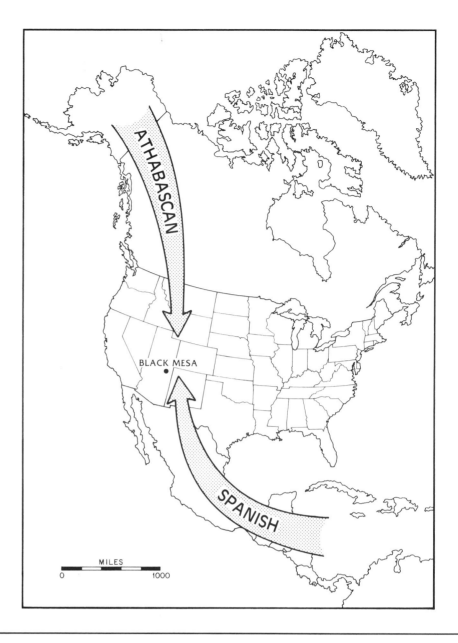

Figure 5-4. The ancestors of the present-day Navajos and Apaches moved into the American Southwest from homelands in the interior of Alaska and Canada. Their language, in the Athabaskan family, was similar to the languages spoken by some of the Athabaskan peoples who still live in Canada and Alaska. A pressing question for archaeologists is when and how they arrived in the Southwest.

and Canada. The Navajos were only one of several groups of Athabaskan speakers who migrated into the area at about the same time. The Apaches, for instance, are also Athabaskan speakers who now live in the American Southwest. A pressing question for archaeologists is how and when the Athabaskan speakers moved from the north into the American Southwest. Three alternative routes have been suggested: east of the Rocky Mountains along the High Plains, through the Rocky Mountains, and through the Great Basin (Figure 5-4). However, there is little archaeological evidence to substantiate any of these alternatives (Box 5-2).

Early southwestern archaeologists thought that nomadic Athabaskan raiders might have been the reason for the extensive Anasazi population relocations of the 1100s and 1200s known collectively as the "abandonment." But since few remains attributed to Athabaskans date earlier than the late 1600s, they probably did not cause the Anasazi abandonments. Spanish documents dating from the mid-1500s through the early 1600s record the presence of nomadic peoples called the Querechos living throughout the territories occupied by Puebloans. But Querecho might have been a name given to all Native Americans who did not live in large stone and adobe pueblos. It is not until the early 1600s that Spanish documents identify the Navajo by name, calling them Apaches de Nabajó.

These Navajos farmed, collected wild plants, and hunted. Early records

indicate that they and their Puebloan neighbors lived in relative harmony. In 1680, the Puebloans rose against the Spanish and forcibly expelled them from New Mexico and Arizona. Fearing eventual reprisals from the Spanish, the Puebloans moved in with Navajos living in the Navajo Reservoir area of northwestern New Mexico (Figure 5-5). At about this same time, the Navajos started accumulating large herds of livestock, the animals being obtained largely from the Spanish by trade and by raiding.

By the mid-1700s, Navajo relations with the Spanish and the Puebloans had deteriorated. Navajos were fighting the Spanish and other Native Americans to defend their territory and to increase their livestock holdings. In 1846, the U.S. Army took over administration of the New Mexico and Arizona territories, but relations with the Navajos did not improve. This period was characterized by extensive slave trading; thousands of Native Americans, including Navajos, were held as slaves in the New Mexico territory by settlers of European descent.

In 1862, Colonel Christopher (Kit) Carson was directed to subjugate the Navajos. Peaceful Navajos were ordered in 1863 to move to Fort Sumner, in east-central New Mexico; but even as this order was being implemented, war was being planned against those Navajos who did not comply. The war began in July 1863 with a "scorched-earth policy"; the Army systematically set fire to the Navajos' fields and buildings, leaving them nothing to eat

Figure 5-5. The Puebloans revolted against their Spanish conquerors in 1680, successfully driving them out of New Mexico and Arizona; many then took refuge with the Navajos living in the Navajo Reservoir district of northwestern New Mexico. These refugee sites (this site is Citadel Ruin) have a curious mixture of Navajo and Puebloan traits, with stone-walled rooms and hogans at the same sites and Puebloan ceramic designs painted on Navajo-style pottery. Photograph by Margaret A. Powers, San Juan County Museum Association, Farmington, New Mexico.

Figure 5-6. Approximately nine thousand Navajos were interned at Fort Sumner in east-central Mexico between 1864 and 1868, and many died while in captivity. Illustration adapted from a National Archives photograph.

and nowhere to hide. They were forced to make the "Long Walk" of over three hundred miles from Fort Defiance in Arizona to Fort Sumner (also called Bosque Redondo) in New Mexico. Over 9,000 Navajos eventually made the trek, with at least 10 percent dying en route (Figure 5-6).

Somewhere between a thousand and two thousand Navajos avoided imprisonment by hiding in remote and inaccessible locations in northern and western Arizona. Legends suggest that the Grand Canyon and Navajo Mountain were two important refuges, and archaeological evidence indicates that northern Black Mesa was a hiding spot for some Navajos during this period.

The Navajos imprisoned at Fort Sumner were freed in 1868, after inhumane conditions had further decimated the population. They were allowed to return to a reservation in northwestern New Mexico and northeastern Arizona that was just a portion of their former homeland. Many, however, returned to homes on non-reservation lands where they had lived before being forced to go to Fort Sumner. The post-internment period was characterized by rapid population growth and the rapid introduction of Euroamerican cultural traits. The economic system came to be dominated by trading posts, whose owners encouraged rug weaving for the tourist trade. Boarding schools were built, and young children were forcibly relo-

cated and raised in an alien culture. The coming of the railroad created construction jobs and broadened the market for Native American arts and crafts. At the same time, livestock holdings increased, and herds came to be one of the dominant forces in Navajo life (Figure 5-7).

By the early 1900s, there was a substantial population living on northern Black Mesa, primarily during the winter. Black Mesa was an ideal wintering spot for people and their herds because of the immense quantities of wood that could be used as fuel. But the growing season was short at Black Mesa's high altitudes, so most people moved north for the summer to the lower elevations of the Kayenta, Long House, and Klethla valleys. In 1918, an influenza epidemic killed at least 6 percent of the Navajos living in northeastern Arizona. Even so, by 1920 local populations were too large to permit seasonal movement, and a number of families established permanent claims to northern Black Mesa, both wintering and summering there.

Navajo lifeways have been characterized by change, especially over the past fifty years. Huge herds of sheep, goats, and cattle, on which the Navajo had come to rely, were forcibly reduced in size by the U.S. government in the late 1930s. Stock reduction increased the Navajos' dependence on outside sources of income, especially off-reservation jobs. Many Navajos fought in World War II, where some were "code-talkers." The Navajo language is so unique and difficult for non-native speakers to understand that radio mes-

Figure 5-7. Herds of sheep, goats, cattle, and horses became an important part of Navajo social and economic life following the Fort Sumner period.

Figure 5-8. The Peabody mines on Black Mesa employ about one thousand people. This man is operating the dragline and clearing overburden in the J1/N6 pit.

sages could be sent and received securely in Navajo with no additional coding.

Peabody Coal Company leased 101 square miles on northern Black Mesa from the Navajo and Hopi tribes in the mid-1960s, and mining operations commenced in 1970. The two mines now employ about 1,000 people, including about 850 Native Americans, primarily Navajos and Hopis. The mining operation has caused a population boom as people are attracted to the wage-labor opportunities. However, much of the land formerly used for grazing, farming, and plant collecting is unavailable to the local people while it is being mined and reclaimed (Figure 5-8).

The Joint Use Area, several hundred square miles of land set aside for the use of Navajos and Hopis in 1882, was partitioned in 1977. Most of that territory had been settled by Navajos, who were forced to move out of those areas given to the Hopis. Much of central and northern Black Mesa was affected, including a small portion of the Peabody lease area (Figure 5-9).

We are aware of the recent history of Black Mesa and the Colorado Plateau because of the recollections of Native Americans and the records kept by the Spanish and Euroamerican conquerers of the region. Many of these events are also documented in the recent archaeological record, including details of human suffering and forbearance not recorded in official

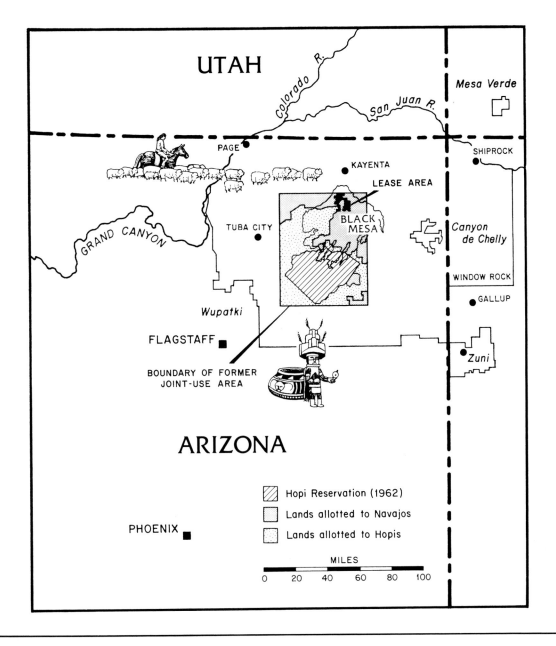

UTAH

Mesa Verde

PAGE

KAYENTA

SHIPROCK

LEASE AREA

BLACK
MESA

TUBA CITY

Canyon
de Chelly

GRAND CANYON

WINDOW ROCK

GALLUP

Wupatki

FLAGSTAFF

BOUNDARY OF FORMER
JOINT-USE AREA

Zuni

ARIZONA

Hopi Reservation (1962)

Lands allotted to Navajos

Lands allotted to Hopis

PHOENIX

MILES

0   20   40   60   80   100

Figure 5-9. The Joint Use Area was established in 1882 for both the Navajo and Hopi tribes. Over the years most of this land came to be used by Navajos, and disputes about land tenure resulted in partitioning of the area in 1977. Navajos living in parts of the former Joint Use Area that were assigned to the Hopi Tribe are being forcibly relocated to new lands.

histories. As the years pass and the events and rich culture of the twentieth-century Black Mesa Navajo become dim memories, archaeology may contribute to documenting a fuller picture of past lifeways and how they changed.

SITE DISCOVERY AND DATA COLLECTION: MAY 1981

The project directors stopped the truck at the base of a low sandstone cliff. They had driven to this spot, just north of Yellow Water Canyon, to try to relocate a Navajo camp that had been found on survey the year before and assigned the number D:7:4089. The camp had been abandoned within the past twenty-five years, which posed a legal quandary for the archaeologists (Box 5-3).

During the project's early history, they had generally avoided the problem of what to do with Navajo sites by doing nothing at all. Since most of the project's archaeologists had been trained to study prehistoric Anasazi remains, the Navajo sites had been pretty much ignored. But during the mid-1970s they had started arguing about what an excavated prehistoric

Box 5-3. Archaeological laws limit their protection to those sites that are legally "significant." In practice, some federal agencies claim that a site must be unique, spectacular, or at least 50 years old. So under the law, site D:7:4089 did not qualify for either protection or excavation. Yet people had lived at the site, and archaeologists claim to be interested in all past human behavior irrespective of when and where it took place.

Figure 5-10. The archaeologists working on prehistoric sites wondered what kind of remains would be left behind by deteriorated but unburned structures. The top photograph shows the remains of an excavated wooden habitation, about one thousand years old, that had burned. The structure was detected by the outline of burned posts. The bottom photograph shows a fifty-year-old Navajo hogan. The question was what, besides the wood, archaeologists would find if they excavated it.

dwelling ought to look like. Some expected to find obvious remains of walls and floors; others thought that the evidence might not be that clear. Masonry rooms and burned wooden rooms left clear remains; but what if a room had been made of wood that had not burned? What might the archaeologists expect to find when they excavated a wooden structure that had deteriorated gradually over several hundred years? Of course, the answer depended on how long the rooms had been used and what the occupants had left behind, but it was becoming clear that long-abandoned structures might have fewer remains than the archaeologists were expecting to find. And if this was the case, they might be missing or misinterpreting many of the things they were excavating on prehistoric sites.

The project directors decided that the Navajo sites might provide some answers to these questions. Most of the structures on Navajo sites were made of wood, most were between a few years and 150 years old, and very few of them had burned. Perhaps most important, most of the structures still had standing wooden superstructures, so there was no question about whether a structure had existed there. All in all, the Navajo sites were ideal for determining what an unburned wooden structure would leave behind (Figure 5-10).

The directors were also concerned about how quickly the way that Navajos were living on northern Black Mesa was changing. Since 1967, when

archaeologists first started working for Peabody Coal Company on northern Black Mesa, the Navajos living there had changed from herders and agriculturalists to wage laborers. True, a few of the older folks still ran sheep and planted crops, but most of the younger people worked for the mines or for the many service industries that had sprung up to provide for the mining operation and its employees (Figure 5-11).

The coal reserves within the Black Mesa lease area were substantial, and the mine-related activities would be in operation until about 2025. By then, the old people would be gone and many of the old ways might be forgotten. Maybe the archaeologists could record and preserve some of this information. The directors thought there were several good reasons for paying more attention to the Navajo archaeological remains within the lease area.

They presented their case to the coal company, which agreed. So, with this moral and financial support behind them, the project directors decided to ignore the difficult-to-interpret federal regulations about what made an archaeological site "significant" enough to warrant data recovery. If Peabody was willing to fund the work, government agencies were unlikely to interfere; and they really could not tell the archaeologists not to do the work, since the sites were probably going to be destroyed by future mining activity anyway.

Unfortunately, with the decision made to place greater emphasis on the

Figure 5-11. The Navajos living on Black Mesa today still depend on herding and agriculture for their living. However, as the coal mines have expanded and as more land is being mined and reclaimed, many of the local people have turned to wage labor to earn a living. Kayenta Motors combines elements from the cash and subsistence economies.

Navajo sites, the directors found that survey information was inconsistent at best and often totally lacking. Survey crews had been trained to identify the smallest Anasazi sites, but they could walk right through a sheep corral and either miss it entirely or misrecord it as a hogan. The directors found that they could not rely on the survey forms to choose sites for excavation. Instead, they selected a sample of likely sites and revisited them to check what was there (Figure 5-12).

The survey crew had found six features on site D:7:4089, and they were located over a huge area. A wood storage area, two lamb pens, a windbreak, a cribbed hogan, a sweatlodge, and a wooden fence were supposed to be situated on the ridge right in front of the truck, but the project directors saw none of these. They knew they shouldn't be discouraged; the site might just be hidden in the pinyon and juniper trees that grew thickly over the ridge. But so far they had had bad luck; some of the survey crews seemed to think that any pile of dead wood was a Navajo structure. The surveyors were just not well enough trained to distinguish natural deadfall wood from wood that had been cut, broken, and stacked by human hands.

There was only one way to tell whether the site was there. Shrugging their shoulders, the two directors got out of the truck and started hiking up the ridge. Immediately their progress was hindered by intertwined broken wood that snaked along the top of the ridge line. It was the fence. They

followed the fence along its entire length, almost half a mile, finding one hogan and one lamb pen. The fence had probably been built to pen livestock in the box canyon below. Whoever had built it had put a lot of effort into it and had probably lived at this place for quite a long time. The directors now knew they had relocated a large habitation site. As they descended the cliff to the floodplain below, they found a stone ring and a stone wall that fenced off a small box canyon. This cinched it. They decided to return to camp and bring the excavation crew out the next day.

In camp the following morning, the excavation crew chief walked out to her pickup truck to check the loading of equipment. Her assistants had put together a site notebook that included all the survey information on site D:7:4089 along with copies of blank forms that would be filled out during excavation. This morning they were loading excavation equipment into the back of the truck along with the transit, the tripod, and the long tape that would be used to map the locations of all the artifacts, features, and structures they found.

Confident that they had all their equipment, notes, food, and water, the five-person crew piled into the truck to follow the project directors out to the site. When they arrived, their first chore was to improve the old road leading to the hogan on the ridge top. It would have been exhausting to carry all their equipment up the face of the cliff every day. While the crew

Figure 5-12. Archaeologists, trained to record remains from prehistoric Anasazi sites, often had problems identifying the remnants of Navajo occupations. The wood in this photograph is all that is left of a dismantled Navajo structure.

Figure 5-13. The crew members combed the site's surface looking for every artifact, structure, and feature. Whenever they found something, they placed a pin flag in the ground to mark its place. Once everything had been flagged, the items were mapped on a large piece of graph paper.

members were doing this, the crew chief accompanied the project directors on a walk-over of the site area. In fact, she was much better informed about Navajo archaeology than the directors and pointed out several structures and features they had walked right by the day before. The survey crew had identified six structures, and the crew chief (with the help of the directors) found eight more.

The crew chief also questioned the 1950 date assigned to the site by the survey crew. By 1950, the Navajos on northern Black Mesa had access to pickup trucks and processed food. Processed foods, especially canned and bottled goods, are bulky and require mechanized transport. Their users also leave behind a lot of discarded bottles and cans. Site D:7:4089 had surprisingly few discarded cans on its surface, particularly in the area surrounding the stone hogan ring and the stone wall that fenced off the small box canyon. The lack of modern debris suggested that at least part of the site had been occupied earlier than 1930, although some of the structures might have been built and used as late as 1950.

With the road cleared and the preliminary reconnaissance completed, the crew chief drove her truck up to a central spot on the site. While her crew unloaded, she selected a point (the datum) from which everything on the site would be mapped. Although provenience is very important on historic as well as on prehistoric sites, the procedures used to record it are dif-

ferent. Navajo sites are so large compared to Anasazi sites that it would be impractical to place a grid over the entire site area. It would take days to lay out a grid, and most of the squares would have nothing in them. A quicker and better alternative was to map the exact location of everything they found. To do this, the transit was set up at the datum. The entire crew combed the site, placing brightly colored pin flags in the ground wherever they found items that needed to be mapped. The pin flags were tall enough and bright enough to be seen from just about anywhere on the site. Once everything was flagged, their angles and distances from the datum were measured and mapped onto a large piece of graph paper. Depending on the number of things found on the site, this procedure could take a couple of hours or several days (Figure 5-13).

The archaeologists readily identified most of the artifacts left on the site. The most common items were beverage and food cans, many with their labels still intact. They noted the type of can, its former contents, its volume, and its exact provenience on an analysis sheet. It takes a huge amount of space to store artifacts, and since little more could be learned from them, most of the cans were not collected. The archaeologists were puzzled by some of the artifacts. These items were mapped and tallied on the analysis sheet, and then they were bagged and returned to the field laboratory for further examination (Figure 5-14).

Figure 5-14. Most of the artifacts found on historic-period sites were readily identified by the archaeologists in the field. Cans, bottles, and other common artifacts were tallied but not collected, since further analysis was unnecessary. Occasionally, however, the archaeologists found an unusual item that defied immediate identification. These artifacts were bagged and taken to the field laboratory for an expert to look at.

Figure 5-15. Almost all Navajo structures on northern Black Mesa were made of wood. The stone hogan, wall, and lamb pen on site D:7:4089 were highly unusual because they were made of stone. Initially the archaeologists thought they had been built at the same time by the same people, but after talking to informants they had to change their minds.

It took a couple of days for the archaeologists to map and tally all the artifacts, features, and structures. When they were done, they had found fourteen structures and features: five windbreaks, two hogans (one made of stone, one of wood), two lamb pens, two sweatlodges, a stone wall that partitioned off the box canyon for use as a corral, the long fence that followed the ridge line, and one small roofed structure that was unlike anything else they had seen.

The different kinds of structures and their relationships to one another suggested that the site had a complex history. Several of the windbreaks (unroofed wooden lean-tos that were built for short-term shelter from the wind and rain during the spring and fall) had east-facing entrances and interior hearths. Since these windbreaks were not alike, they were probably built by different people at different times. The wooden hogan stood by itself at the top of the ridge. Hogans are far more substantial shelters than windbreaks, so this lone hogan was probably built and used separately from the windbreaks. Finally, the stone hogan ring, the stone wall, and one stone lamb pen were all clustered together in the small box canyon. Their location next to one another and the fact that they were all built of stone (an unusual construction material for Black Mesa Navajo sites) suggested that these three structures had been built and used by the same people at the same time (Figure 5-15).

The archaeologists had trouble determining who had built the rest of the structures and features and when they had been used. Sweatlodges, often used for ritual purification, are built at some distance from other structures on an inhabited site. This meant that proximity to one or the other hogan was not good evidence of when the sweatlodges had been used. The only cultural materials found near the sweatlodges were piles of burned, heat-cracked sandstone. The rocks had been heated in a fire outside the sweatlodge and then placed inside to provide a smokeless heat source. Their presence confirmed that the small structures were sweatlodges, but unfortunately there was no way to date the rocks.

The long, ridge-top fence was probably built by the occupants of the wooden hogan and extended by subsequent inhabitants of the site. The hogan would have been built for a fairly lengthy stay, one that probably focused on the movement of livestock. The long fence would have penned the animals in the box canyon. The lamb pen built into the fence line confirmed that the fence had been used to corral livestock. Lambs too young to follow the herd were placed in the lamb pens each morning when the herder took the rest of the flock out to graze, so these pens were located right next to where the herds were penned for the night (Figure 5-16).

The small roofed structure was a strange one. There was a hearth inside, suggesting that the structure had been built and used during the cold

Figure 5-16. Lamb pens were small enclosures built into corrals. During the spring, after the lambs were born, the herder separated them from the rest of the flock and placed them in the pens. This practice kept the lambs safe and allowed the rest of the herd to graze unimpeded by the immature animals.

weather. It was not as well built as a hogan, but considerably more effort had gone into its construction than into a windbreak. Perhaps the strange structure had been used as a habitation while the hogan was being built. But this was guesswork; the archaeologists were just not sure.

The mapping and artifact collecting had answered many questions about the site (Figure 5-17), but two remained. First, although the archaeologists were fairly sure that some of the structures had been built and used at the same time and that they all predated 1950, there was no conclusive evidence about when they had been built. Second, they were curious about what the excavated structures might look like in comparison to excavated Anasazi structures.

There were two ways to try to find out when the structures had been built. One was to find people who had lived at the site and ask them; the other was to collect tree-ring samples from the wooden structures and have them analyzed. However, there were limits to both of these potential sources of information.

An informant, someone who had lived at the site or knew about the site, was limited by his or her memory. People forget the answers to many of the mundane questions in which the archaeologists would be interested. In addition, people can recall only those things that happened to them or that they heard about during their lifetimes. Since this particular site had been

built before 1950 and possibly before 1930, a person who knew about the earliest occupation firsthand would now (in 1981) be well over fifty years old. It was unlikely that many people would still be around who could tell of sites that had been occupied much before 1930; and even if there were such people to be found, they might not be willing to talk to archaeologists. Many people prefer not to talk to outsiders about their personal recollections, and the archaeologists respected their right to feel this way. Nonetheless, they found three men—aged forty-eight, fifty-six, and eighty—who had lived at the site and were willing to talk about it. Their stories come later.

Despite the good luck of finding willing informants, the archaeologists still collected tree-ring samples. Even the best of informants was unlikely to remember everything, much less the exact year that everything on the site happened; and sometimes even the best-intentioned informant gives incorrect information. The tree-ring analysis was one way to fill in missing information and to verify the informants' recollections.

Collecting tree-ring samples was a relatively simple matter. Most of the structures had been made of wood, and much wood remained. The archaeologists used a small handsaw to cut sections from several pieces of wood from each structure. The tricky part was to find wood that had been live-cut especially for building that particular structure. The Black Mesa Navajos,

Figure 5-17. An archaeologist maps the locations of artifacts, structures, and features as they are found. The field map helps the archaeologists plan appropriate strategies for each phase of the excavation.

Figure 5-18. The archaeologists collected wood samples for tree-ring dating from all the structures and features with suitable wood. The choice of samples was tricky, since the Navajos reused wood from abandoned structures whenever possible. The archaeologists had to be careful to select samples from wood that had been cut especially for that particular structure. Otherwise they might get the date of an older structure from which wood had been reclaimed or of a long-dead tree whose wood had been used.

even though they lived in a comparatively wood-rich environment, were frugal in their use of wood. It was hard work cutting and trimming wood with hand tools, and the work had been even harder before the common use of steel tools after the Fort Sumner period in the late 1860s. If people were building new structures, and there was an abandoned structure with suitable old wood nearby, they would reuse the old wood wherever possible. And, even more common, they used deadwood—often hundreds of years old. However sensible and understandable, this practice created problems for the archaeologists, who wanted to date the structure being sampled, not the previous structures from which old wood was taken (Figure 5-18).

The archaeologists had found that despite this pattern of wood reuse, certain new wooden elements had to be cut for almost any structure. The support posts and crossbeam for a hogan's doorway were almost always cut just for the new structure; old wood was unlikely to be exactly the right size. And although lots of deadwood scavenged from other sources was used in corrals, the small pieces of wood and brush used to chink the gaps between the larger pieces were almost always newly cut. With this information in mind, the archaeologists carefully examined the wood in each structure or feature, avoiding pieces that looked much older or otherwise different from the rest of the wood.

The excavations proceeded much like excavations of prehistoric sites, but with one or two major differences. First, most of the structures were still standing, so there was little trouble in figuring out where to dig. The interior of each structure and two to four yards surrounding the walls were excavated. Since there had been so little time for the features and structures to become buried, almost everything lay right beneath a shallow layer of blow sand. So the digging went quickly, and there were few surprises.

As on prehistoric sites, if the archaeologists dug only where they saw evidence of structures and features, they might miss things that had been completely buried. To avoid this problem, a "probabilistic" element was introduced to the excavations. The archaeologists dug a series of test squares at points selected with a random number table. Two numbers were chosen: one (between 1 and 360) represented the angle from the north line; the second represented the distance from datum. The combination of the two identified a unique point that was so many degrees from north and so many meters from the datum. Fifty points were chosen, and a 2 × 2−meter square was dug to a depth of at least eight inches. The fill from each hole was examined for charcoal and artifacts, which were totally lacking in forty-eight of the fifty. Since the other two test holes had some charcoal, a larger area was excavated around each, but nothing was found.

The archaeologists then turned their attention to excavating the structures. A 1 × 1−meter grid was superimposed over each structure and the

Figure 5-19. The archaeologists divided the structure and the area immediately surrounding it into 1 × 1–meter squares. Excavation of historic structures was very similar to excavation of prehistoric structures, except that on the more recent sites most things were found just below the ground's surface.

area immediately surrounding it. After it had been mapped, the excavators carefully cleared fallen wood and stones from the areas to be excavated; deadwood and loose stones were favored homes for rattlesnakes, and almost all crew members who worked on Navajo sites had stories to tell of encounters with the "buzz-worms."

Once the grid was established and the debris cleared away, excavation proceeded exactly as it would on a prehistoric site. The archaeologists excavated within the 1 × 1–meter units, and all artifacts and samples from each vertical level were bagged together. A structure's floor, any floor features, and the artifacts were generally found right under the sand that had blown into the structure since it had been abandoned. However, a small trench was always extended below the living surface so the archaeologists could see how the cultural activity had changed the soil profiles. This information was valuable for comparing soil profiles on historic sites with those on prehistoric sites. Ideally, similar-looking profiles had been produced by similar activities; so prehistoric profiles that matched historic ones might be interpreted with more assurance than was possible without the information from the historic excavations (Figure 5-19).

In general, the excavations did not tell the archaeologists much more than could be determined from the site's surface. They found no new structures or features, but they did learn what the remains from unburned structures might look like if there was no wood left to mark their locations. In structures like the windbreaks that had been lived in for only short periods of time, there was no clear demarcation where the floor had been. The blow sand was much softer than the undisturbed soil on which the structure had been built, but both the sand and the undisturbed soil were the same color. Texture and density (how hard-packed the soil was) were the two characteristics that distinguished the presence of the structure.

The excavators working on site D:7:4089 found that many of the wooden support posts had been removed, leaving only a hole that had been filled in by sand but no charcoal or charred wood (Box 5-4). There were no striking differences in color between the fill and the undisturbed soil. They could determine that posts had been present only by differences in soil texture and density.

Hearths and ashpits were also excavated. These features were clearly distinguishable on the surface as dark soil stains, and the excavators collected artifacts, large bones, and flotation samples from them. The bones and the floral remains recovered from the flotation samples would tell the archaeologists about the foods cooked and discarded by the site's inhabitants.

All in all, the excavations did not provide much more information about

Box 5-4. Archaeologists working on prehistoric sites often define a structure by the presence of postholes, small cylindrical depressions in which posts were set. If the structure burned, archaeologists generally find remnants of the burned post; and even if they don't, the posthole is distinguishable by the dark soil and charcoal that has accumulated in the hole over the years.

how the site had been used than could be gleaned from its surface. However, it had been worth the time and trouble just to answer questions about what the remains of unburned prehistoric structures might look like.

The archaeologists followed four major steps in their investigation of the Navajo site: site mapping, artifact collection, excavations of the structures, and collection of tree-ring samples. With these data collected and with the artifacts identified, they knew as much about this site as they would about any of the prehistoric sites. The structures and features clustered into three groups, groups that shared other similarities besides proximity. The string of windbreaks (including the strangely roofed structure) along the ridge top were all alike in size, in orientation of doorways, and in having hearths. However, the particulars of how they had been built suggested that different people had designed and built each one. The second group, the wood hogan and the ridge-line fence, were both built of wood. The hogan was a far more substantial shelter than the windbreaks, meaning it had probably been used for a longer period of time and through the cold winter months. The structures of the third cluster—the stone hogan, the wall, and the lamb pen—were all built in the box canyon at the foot of the ridge. This unique construction style and location suggested that this part of the site had been built and used at the same time by the same people.

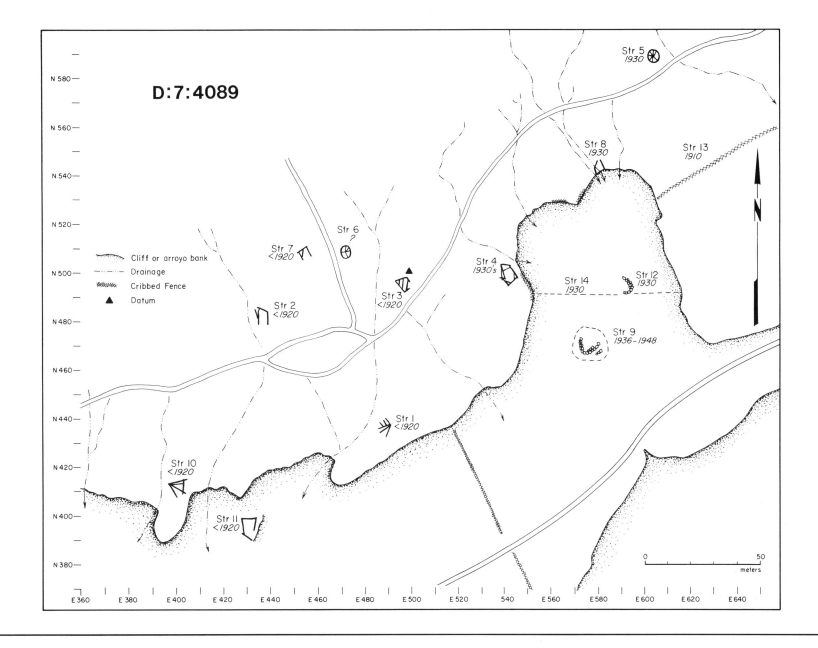

There were few artifacts, and they were all made before 1950. In general, discarded artifacts had been dumped well away from the living areas of the site; people do not want to live in their own trash. The artifacts, therefore, provided little information about how the various structures and features had been used. Instead, they reinforced the archaeologists' interpretation that the site, as a whole, had been occupied off-and-on from the turn of the century until about 1950 (Figure 5-20).

The tree-ring samples yielded confusing results. The sample with the earliest date, 1538, was from one of the windbreaks, but it was far too old for a Black Mesa Navajo site and probably came from deadwood. The other two samples from this same windbreak dated to 1835 and 1838; these dates also seemed early, but the archaeologists accepted them because they were so close together. Most of the remaining samples dated between the turn of the century and 1948, reinforcing the information gained from the artifacts. However, the archaeologists could not discount the earlier dates of 1835 and 1838. Navajos occupying sites that long ago would not have used Euroamerican items like cans and bottles that leave so many durable remains. Most of their tools would have been made from perishable materials and thus would have left no remains. So at least part of the site had probably been occupied in the mid-1800s.

Figure 5-20. Site D:7:4089 consisted of many widely scattered structures built over many years by many different people.

Figure 5-21. (above and far right). Traditional economic pursuits for the lease area's inhabitants included sheep herding, agriculture, hunting, plant collecting, and craft production. More recently people have raised cattle and worked for archaeologists and businesses attracted by the coal mining.

Archaeologists working with prehistoric materials often come up with interpretations that are this iffy, which is why the results of prehistoric excavations are often so unsatisfying. The prehistoric archaeologists know what they have found, but often they do not know what it means. Indeed, often they cannot make even the simplest statements about the number of people who lived at a site, when they lived there, and what they were doing while they were there. The excavators of site D:7:4089 would be in much the same boat if they had had no further sources of information. Fortunately for them, however, some of the crew members knew who had lived at site D:7:4089, and arrangements were made for the archaeologists to talk with the site's former occupants.

WHAT INFORMANTS SAID ABOUT SITE D:7:4089

Before the mine-related population boom that began in the early 1970s, only Navajos lived within the lease area. Approximately two hundred people, belonging to twelve extended families, grazed their sheep, planted fields, hunted, and collected wild plants (Figure 5-21). The Hopi Tribe also made legal claim to the southern half of the lands leased and mined by Peabody Coal Company, but no Hopis actually lived in the lease area.

The legalities of land tenure were reflected in the choice of crew members by the archaeological project. Each of the Navajo camps claimed sole grazing rights to large tracts of land, land that Peabody was mining and that the archaeologists wished to survey and perhaps excavate. Although Peabody could grant legal permission for the archaeologists to work on the land, the local residents had had no voice in the matter. Peabody's lease agreements were negotiated directly with official tribal representatives, and often the local residents had little or no information about what was happening to their lands and why.

Over the years Peabody had established an office of environmental affairs; and one of the people who worked for this office, a Navajo woman who lived in Kayenta, was responsible for relations between the coal company and the local residents. The archaeologists worked with this woman to find out whose land they would be working on, to arrange access to the land, and to determine who should be hired to work on the archaeological field and laboratory crews.

Although some people belonging to each of the camps had been hired by the coal company, many others spoke little or no English or were too old or too young to work in the highly industrialized surface mining operation. These were the people who generally were most dependent on traditional economic pursuits like herding and agriculture, the same economic activi-

Figure 5-22. All of the Black Mesa project's crews consisted of Native Americans and Euroamericans. Here, a Navajo woman, a Hopi man, and a Euroamerican man prepare to start work on a Navajo site.

ties most affected by the mining operation. To reduce the negative impact of the mining on these people, arrangements were made for them to be employed by the archaeological project. These arrangements were formalized in the archaeologists' work permits, which required that all nonprofessional personnel be Native Americans.

Even though they had not lived within the lease since their ancestors abandoned the area at about A.D. 1150, the Hopis, too, had a legal claim to some of the leased lands. So the archaeological project hired Hopis as well as Navajos to work in the field and the laboratory. This relationship was beneficial to the local people, but it was even more beneficial to the archaeologists. The Navajos were an inexhaustible source of information about local conditions—including where sites were located—as well as about the specifics of the historic-period occupation of the area. And although the Hopis were not as familiar with local conditions as the Navajos, they had descended from the Anasazi and many of their cultural practices were still very similar to those of the Anasazi. Thus the Hopis were an invaluable source of information for interpreting the prehistoric sites.

The crew included Euroamerican students from the University of New Mexico and Southern Illinois University, a Navajo boy, a middle-aged Navajo woman, and a Hopi man from Second Mesa (Figure 5-22). The Navajo boy lived just upstream from site D:7:4089; by hiring him the project en-

sured that the crew would have no problems gaining access to the site. His family's grazing area had been fenced, and a locked gate barred entry to the site area. Each morning the boy met the rest of the crew at the gate, unlocking it for the truck to drive through and then relocking it behind the archaeologists. The procedure operated in reverse every afternoon after work; so the archaeologists were able to drive to the site, and the family was reassured that the gate would remain closed and their livestock would not escape.

While they were working on site D:7:4089, the Navajo boy volunteered that his father had lived there during the 1930s as a boy, but he was not sure which of the structures his father had lived in. This information initiated a heated lunchtime discussion about which of the structures might have been built in the 1930s and whether the other structures were older or younger than that.

As a girl, the woman crew member had lived downstream from D:7:4089, where Yazzie Wash drains into Yellow Water Canyon (Figure 5-23). After she married, she had moved to her husband's family's grazing area, several miles away from site D:7:4089 in the eastern part of the lease area. She thought she remembered that her maternal aunt and the aunt's family had lived in the general vicinity of site D:7:4089 at about the same time she moved away. Her aunt had died some time ago, but her aunt's husband was

Figure 5-23. Navajo settlements on northern Black Mesa consisted of several buildings and corrals. Often they were built on floodplains where two major washes came together.

still alive. She believed he was living with his family down in Long House Valley, and thought he might be willing to visit site D:7:4089 and share what he knew about the history of the area.

The boy's father and the woman's uncle were each contacted, first by the boy and the woman to make sure they were willing to talk with the archaeologists, and then by the archaeologists themselves to arrange a time to take them to site D:7:4089. They were paid for their time at the same rate as the crew members; usually the travel and the time actually spent on the site took a half day or more.

The site supervisor met the boy and his father at 8:15 on a Saturday morning by the gate to their grazing area. It had been difficult to arrange a time to meet because the boy's father was a third-shift dragline operator and slept during the day after he got off work. But he had been pleased to be asked about the site's history and was eager to talk with the archaeologists. The three drove to site D:7:4089 and walked to all the structures. The boy's father said he had lived at site D:7:4089 with his father and grandparents for about twelve years starting around 1930. The ridge-top windbreaks and one sweatlodge were already there when he, his father, and his grandparents first moved to site D:7:4089. They built the wooden cribbed-log hogan and the stone wall that formed the sheep corral in the box canyon. Later they built the stone hogan and one of the sweatlodges, and added to

the stock fence. The three-generation family used site D:7:4089 as their winter home and herded both sheep and horses at the site. His recollections implied three major clusters of structures at site D:7:4089: the original windbreaks and one of the sweatlodges; the cribbed-log hogan and the stone wall; and the stone hogan, the stock fence, and the other sweatlodge.

That Saturday, the site supervisor and the woman crew member drove to a homestead in Long House Valley, just north of the mesa (Figure 5-24). They were to meet the woman's uncle there, and she had come along to show the way and to translate for her uncle, who spoke little English. When they drove up to his home, they had a surprise. The woman's uncle, who himself was almost sixty, had invited his eighty-year-old father to come along. Apparently his father, too, had lived at site D:7:4089, but even before the uncle had. Between them, the two men were able to identify many of the site D:7:4089 structures.

The woman's uncle claimed to have lived in the stone hogan around 1928 with his grandmother. The hogan was their winter home, and they herded sheep from the site. The sheep were kept in the box canyon, which was unfenced at the time; they did not build the stone fence. The only other structure he was able to identify was one of the windbreaks, which had been constructed by his father as a winter herding camp. That windbreak had been situated on the south-facing slope to catch the winter morning

Figure 5-24. Long House Valley, just north of Black Mesa, is home to many Navajos, some of whom lived on Black Mesa in the past. Black Mesa forms the southern (left) boundary of the valley, and Skeleton Mesa bounds the valley on the north (right).

Figure 5-25 (above and far right). Because Black Mesa is higher and wetter than surrounding areas, pinyon and juniper forests grew there. People came from miles around to collect pinyon nuts and to gather wood for heating and building.

sun. The stock fence and most of the windbreaks were already present when he and his grandparents moved to site D:7:4089, and the wooden hogan and the sweatlodges must have been built after they moved away from the site.

The man's father recalled having built the stock fence around 1910, and his recollections about the stone hogan and the windbreak matched his son's; he remembered building the windbreak about 1920 during the winter. The other windbreaks were already there when the old man first moved to site D:7:4089; he thought they had been built by pinyon nut pickers, since the site was situated in a large, dense stand of pinyon trees.

When queried about why he and his son now lived off the mesa in Long House Valley, the old man recalled that they had never lived on Black Mesa year-round. During the early part of the century, his family would move with their livestock onto Black Mesa for the winter. The mesa top was relatively uninhabited then, and there had never been a problem in finding a place to live for the winter and to graze their animals. However, over the years more and more people had moved onto the mesa, and there was no longer enough land for everyone. Finally, they decided to stay year-round in the valley, although they would camp on the mesa for a couple of weeks in the fall to collect pinyon nuts and cut wood for fuel (Figure 5-25).

The three informants' recollections did not contradict the archaeological

findings in any substantial way, and the informants did help to clarify the relationship between the windbreaks, the stock fence, and the rest of the site. Apparently, the area around site D:7:4089 had first been used for a couple of weeks each year during the pinyon nut harvest—perhaps as early as the 1830s. The stock fence had been built before any of the hogans because they needed a safe place to pen their livestock before many sheep could graze there regularly. There was an apparent discrepancy about who had built the stone hogan; whereas the first informant claimed that his family had built and lived in the stone hogan in the 1930s, the second and third informants stated that it had been built by them in the late 1920s. The crew talked about this problem the following week over lunches while they finished work on site D:7:4089. They thought that maybe both stories were correct: that the old man had built the original stone hogan, and that the other had rebuilt it ten or more years later.

On the final day of work on site D:7:4089, the crew members had a picnic lunch celebration and invited the three informants and the lab workers who had analyzed their artifacts. Pot-luck site parties had become a tradition among the crews working on historic sites, and everyone brought a special food item to help celebrate the end of work. They all contributed some money to purchase a small lamb, and the lamb was placed in a pit barbecue near the site first thing that morning. The Hopi man brought piki

Figure 5-26 (above). Picnic parties to celebrate the end of work at the site were a tradition. Each crew member contributed something to the menu, and all enjoyed the leisurely picnic lunch and conversations about what they had found.

Figure 5-27 (right). The coal, whose presence had brought so many changes to the people of Black Mesa, was being burned to provide electrical power to the large cities of the desert west. The photograph shows the Glen Canyon Dam, Lake Powell, Arizona.

bread, the Navajo woman made fry bread, lab workers brought potato salad in an ice-filled cooler, the student archaeologist brought a case of soft drinks, and the site supervisor made a chocolate cake (Figure 5-26).

They worked straight through until the early afternoon, when they stopped for a leisurely lunch. Just by coincidence, the project directors stopped by as the lamb was being taken out of the barbecue. They were invited to stay for a while, and the food looked so good that they accepted the invitation. They all filled their plates and sat in the shade of a large juniper tree to eat. The conversation centered on the work and what they had learned about site D:7:4089.

Much of the history of the Navajo occupation of northern Black Mesa was recorded in the remains left at site D:7:4089, and what the crew found most startling was how quickly things had changed. The number of people living in the area had grown dramatically, and this population increase was accompanied by many other changes. The earliest series of occupations of site D:7:4089, by pinyon nut pickers, had spanned seventy or eighty years, from the 1830s to the early 1900s. Soon after that, people had started using site D:7:4089 for winter herding camps. Then year-round occupation of the area began, and herds were grazed and crops grown in the floodplain of Yellow Water Canyon. Now the Navajos in the vicinity of site D:7:4089 depended on the large surface coal mines for a living. From where they were

Figure 5-28. The improved accessibility of the northern part of the Navajo Reservation has drawn tourists to the area. Sales of art and craft items and tourist attendance at tribal and intertribal fairs are continuing sources of income. Painting of the Gallup Intertribal Fair by Beatien Yazz, reproduced courtesy of the School of American Research.

sitting, the crew could see the stark profiles of the Kayenta Mine N7-8 pit spoils. It seemed impossible that there had ever been a life without the coal mines and equally impossible that the mining would ever end; yet they all knew that the coal would not last forever.

The coal was being mined so that the people living in the large cities of the desert west could maintain the lifestyle to which they were accustomed, a lifestyle including air-conditioning in the summer, central heating in the winter, and electricity to power all their appliances (Figure 5-27). It was contradictory but true that in order to maintain their own lifestyle and culture, the people of Phoenix, Tucson, and other large western cities were the cause of all the recent changes on northern Black Mesa. Yet the Black Mesa coal would last only thirty or forty years; after that, new energy sources would have to be found or the lifestyle of the city dwellers would have to change (Figure 5-28). No one asked the question aloud, but it was in the air: what would people on Black Mesa be doing then?

EPILOGUE: THE FUTURE

People often ask us as archaeologists to play an intriguing "what if" game. They want to know how future archaeologists would interpret contemporary cultures in the absence of written records. Archaeologists enjoy this game because it allows them to think more realistically about their interpretations of the past.

Some elements of contemporary Black Mesa would prove difficult to decipher archaeologically, while others would not be so hard. It would be fairly easy to determine that mining and reclamation had taken place. The abandoned mine buildings and equipment as well as the changed landscape would provide ample evidence that the land had been disturbed by a massive operation. The existence of non-native grasses and the remains of new animal species would indicate a concern for the environment. The house trailers of the mine's employees, the stores, and the service businesses that grew up in response to the mine would document the population growth and economic prosperity that accompanied the mining operation. But could the many different cultural groups brought together on Black Mesa by the mining be identified from their remains? Could Navajo dwellings be distinguished from Hopi and Euroamerican homes? And what would future archaeologists think of the temporary, ramshackle archaeological camp? Today it is kiddingly called a ghetto, and they would probably agree with that interpretation.

In all probability the homes of Black Mesa's inhabitants will become more and more alike, and more westernized. Future archaeologists would probably interpret the end of hogan building and the appearance of western structures as the end of an old way of life and the beginning of a new one (Figure E-1).

Without written records there would be little evidence of our activities. The archaeological sites themselves will have been destroyed by the mining. Evidence of the concern about the past that led to the enormous archaeological undertaking exists solely on the printed page and in the minds of those administrators and archaeologists who know that the past can tell us something about the future.

Much more difficult than determining how archaeologists in the future would interpret the present is the use of the very recent past to predict the future. Self-styled futurologists are notoriously poor predictors. They tend to use existing trends and simply project future conditions. Innovations, however, cannot be anticipated or predicted. More than anybody, archaeologists, with their extremely long-term view, can observe the impact of innovations. But because the problems of extrapolating from the present to the future are enormous, we make no attempt to predict details of long-term social change in northeastern Arizona. We can, however, offer a few predictions about short-term change.

Figure E-1. Coal mining on Black Mesa has introduced a flood of Euroamerican cultural traits to the area, producing a mixture of the "traditional" and the "modern." An example, this rug, presents mining motifs—a dragline and the Peabody Coal Company logo—in a traditional context. Rug woven by Betty Crank.

Obviously, both the natural and social settings will be different from to-day's. Where mining and reclamation have altered the landscape, rolling grassland will predominate. If the cycle of precipitation continues in the manner that reconstructions of the past environment predict, and if present trends toward cattle-raising and conservation techniques continue, there should be thicker ground cover and less erosion. With more and different grasses, the number and variety of birds and animals should increase in the near future. If the payroll dollars continue to flow, stores, motels, and service stations will proliferate. This economic growth will accelerate the integration of the people of northeastern Arizona into the social and economic network of the state and the nation.

More important than the details about future change in the Black Mesa region are those more general truths provided by an archaeological perspective. No society remains static; cultural fortunes ebb and flow. Innovations provide opportunities and challenges. But change may also lead to cultural evolutionary deadends and contribute to the extinction of a way of life. Archaeology and history are the collective memories of humanity; the Black Mesa studies and others like them provide our best long-term hope of learning from the past.

SUGGESTED READINGS

GLOSSARY

INDEX

SUGGESTED READINGS

Ambler, J. Richard
  1977   *The Anasazi.* Museum of Northern Arizona, Flagstaff.

Canby, Thomas Y.
  1982   The Anasazi: Riddles in the Ruins. *National Geographic* Vol. 162, No. 5,
    pp. 562–605.

Cordell, Linda S.
  1984   *Prehistory of the Southwest.* Academic Press, New York.

Downs, James F.
  1972   *The Navajo.* Holt, Rinehart and Winston, Inc., New York.

Dyk, Walter (recorder)
  1938   *Son of Old Man Hat: A Navaho Autobiography.* University of Nebraska Press,
    Lincoln.

Gaede, Marnie (editor)
  1980   *Camera, Spade and Pen: An Inside View of Southwestern Archaeology.* Univer-
    sity of Arizona Press, Tucson.

Gumerman, George J.
  1984   *A View from Black Mesa: The Changing Face of Archaeology.* University of Ari-
    zona Press, Tucson.

Jones, Dewitt, and Linda S. Cordell
  1985   *Anasazi World.* Graphic Arts Center Publishing Company, Portland, Oregon.

Kelley, Klara B.

1986   *Navajo Land Use: An Ethnoarchaeological Study.* Academic Press, New York.

Muench, David, and Donald G. Pike

1974   *Anasazi: Ancient People of the Rock.* American West Publishing Company, Palo Alto, California.

Noble, David Grant (editor)

1986   *Tse' Yaa Kin: Houses Beneath the Rock.* School of American Research, Santa Fe.

Spicer, Edward H.

1962   *Cycles of Conquest: The Impact of Spain, Mexico, and the United States on the Indians of the Southwest, 1533–1960.* University of Arizona Press, Tucson.

GLOSSARY

absolute date: measurements of time in real calendar years. Absolute dates may be contrasted with "relative dates," which tell archaeologists only that something is older or younger than something else— but not how much older or younger. Radiocarbon and tree-ring samples yield absolute dates; artifacts yield relative dates. In the American Southwest, however, pottery has been dated independently, and distinct ceramic types have been assigned dates in real calendar years. *See also* independent date *and* ceramic type.

arroyo: a gully, or erosional channel, that forms at the bottom of a wash when environmental conditions are dry and the water table is low.

artifact density: the total number of artifacts divided by the amount of area in which they were found. For example, if twenty-seven pieces of broken pottery were found inside a ten-square-meter area, the ceramic density would be 2.7 per square meter. These calculations can be made for all artifacts combined or separately for pottery, chipped stone, or groundstone.

ashpile: trash areas found at Navajo residential sites. They are called ashpiles because the ashes from each day's fire were cleaned from the hearth and dumped in one place along with other kinds of trash.

assemblage: artifacts that were found together and presumably used at the same time for similar or related tasks.

associated (items): artifacts, structures, and/or features that were found together and presumably used together. Sometimes, however, items found close together were not used together. For example, broken pottery thrown inside a collapsed pithouse does not tell the archaeologists anything about who lived in the pithouse or how it was used; therefore, the pottery is not associated with the pithouse. Archaeologists must be careful to look for clues that tell them whether items are associated.

base camp: a camp occupied for long periods of time and used as a residential base. Hunter-gatherers moved seasonally, following available plants and game. During their moves, they lived in a variety of different camps, some occupied for only a few hours or days while performing a specific activity. Base camps, however, were occupied for longer periods of time for a greater variety of activities.

base map: a map of a site that is used for plotting information about artifact densities, feature and structure locations, and ground contours.

bell-shaped pit: a hole, dug into the ground, with a narrow opening that flares out into a spherical pit. The name comes from the profile, which looks like a bell. The walls of the pit were often fired to harden them and to kill any insects and larvae that might be present. Food was probably stored in these pits. *See also* storage pit.

biface: a tool shaped from a larger flake or blade by carefully removing flakes from both front and back. The flakes removed during the final shaping are called biface thinning flakes.

biface thinning flakes: the small flakes removed during the final shaping of a biface.

carbonize: to burn and char organic remains, leaving a blackened (carbonized) residue. Things that have been carbonized are much less susceptible to decay, and thus tend to survive well at many archaeological sites.

ceramic type: a category of pottery made from the same kind of clay decorated in similar ways. Usually all the pottery belonging to a single ceramic type was made in the same area during the same period of time.

chipped stone: flakes of stone with sharp edges, used for cutting, scraping, or drilling—although the waste flakes (left over after chipped stone tools have been made) are also called chipped stone. The best known chipped stone tools are arrowheads and spear points.

cist: a rectangular, sandstone-lined hole dug into the ground. Food and other items were stored in the cist, which was then sealed with another sandstone slab placed over its top. Old cists were sometimes used as burial crypts during Basketmaker times. *See also* storage pit.

component: a single occupation by one group at a location that was also used at other times by different groups of people. The different components of a site have nothing to do with one another except that they were constructed at the same location.

core (lithic): the piece of stone from which chipped stone flakes are struck. When the core is so small that no more flakes can be removed from it, it is said to be "exhausted."

culturally sterile soil: soil that shows no signs of human disturbance. Culturally sterile soil is usually uniformly hard-packed (because no one has dug into it) and has no charcoal or artifacts in it.

datum: the single point, usually marked by a securely placed stake, used for measuring items in space on an archaeological site. The datum may be located on the site itself (in which case the archaeologists must be careful not to disturb it during excavations), or it may be located off the site. *See also* provenience.

daub: mud or clay used to plaster and seal houses made of sticks and poles. *See also* jacal.

dendrochronology: the study of tree rings to determine when trees germinated and died. Dendrochronology, or tree-ring dating, tells archaeologists when wooden construction beams were cut, which in turn tells them when a structure was built.

diagnostic (artifact): an artifact that tells the archaeologists something about who made it and when it was made. Painted pottery, arrowheads, and spear points are often diagnostic artifacts. *See also* temporally sensitive.

enamel hypoplasias: lines on teeth, parallel with the gum line, where enamel failed to form. Enamel hypoplasias are most commonly caused by poor diet and by disease.

ethnobotany: the study of plant remains and of how plants were used by modern and prehistoric peoples.

extended family: a multigeneration family whose members, often including parents, grandparents, and children, live together.

feature: site fixtures that are too small to be structures. Commonly found features include hearths, roasting pits, and storage pits.

fill: the soil, charcoal, ash, and artifacts found inside structures and features.

fire: to subject to intense direct or indirect heat. Pottery is intentionally fired to harden the clay, but many other things found on archaeological sites were fired accidentally when they burned. Firing, whether intentional or accidental, helps to preserve many items by hardening or carbonizing them.

flake: a chip of stone intentionally broken from a larger piece of stone. Stone flakes have definite characteristics (including sharp edges and a "platform" where the flake was struck from the larger piece) that allow archaeologists to identify them.

flotation sample: a measured amount of soil, usually two to four quarts, that is collected from structures, features, and middens. In the laboratory the soil is placed in water, and the lighter-than-water materials (the light fraction) are skimmed off the water's surface. The light fraction consists of seeds, plant remains, and other organic materials that are identified by botanists. Flotation samples are a way that archaeologists can recover materials that cannot be seen in the soil and that are too small to be recovered by screening.

groundstone: stone tools shaped by pecking and grinding. The groundstone tools most commonly found on northern Black Mesa sites were used for milling corn and other seeds. *See also* mano *and* metate.

growth arrest lines: lines perpendicular to the long axis that show up on X-rays of human arm and leg bones. Growth arrest lines are areas of densely packed bone cells caused by poor nutrition, disease, and other stresses. Another name for growth arrest lines is Harris lines.

haft: to set a tool, usually a spear or arrow point, into a shaft. Archaeologists usually find no evidence of how a point was hafted into its shaft.

Harris lines: *see* growth arrest lines.

hogan: a Navajo dwelling. Hogans are usually circular with east-facing doorways. Because the hogan played an important mythical role in the creation of the Navajo homeland (Dinetah) and the Navajo people, the form and orientation of hogans are dictated by Navajo origin myths.

independent date: a date that has been substantiated by dates from materials other than the item in question. For example, a piece of pottery from the floor of a burned pithouse may be independently dated by tree-ring samples from the structure's roof. *See also* absolute date.

jacal: a structure made of poles and thatch plastered with mud or clay. *See also* daub.

Kachinas: supernatural beings who have the power to bring rain and other good things to the Puebloans.

kiva: a ceremonial structure used by modern and prehistoric Puebloans. Kivas are usually (but not always) circular; they are subterranean and house a symbolic sipapu, or mythical entrance to the underworld. *See also* sipapu.

lease area: the 101-square-mile area on northern Black Mesa leased by Peabody Coal Company from the Navajo and Hopi tribes. Much of the leased land will be strip-mined for coal.

lithic: made of stone. Usually archaeologists use the term "lithic" to refer to chipped stone tools.

mano: a groundstone tool held in the hand and used to crush or grind corn and other seeds. Mano is the Spanish word for hand. *See also* groundstone.

metate: a large, flat, basin- or trough-shaped groundstone tool. Corn and other seeds are placed on the metate and then crushed and ground with the mano. *See also* groundstone.

midden: the place on a site where household trash and broken artifacts were dumped. Most human burials are found in middens on prehistoric Black Mesa sites, perhaps because the ground was soft and easy to dig.

mobility: frequent movement over the landscape, usually in response to the seasonal availability of food. Hunters and gatherers are quite mobile, agriculturalists much less so.

natural level: a soil layer that can be clearly distinguished by a change in color or texture or by the presence of artifacts and charcoal. When archaeologists are unable to distinguish natural levels during excavation, they dig in arbitrary levels that are generally two to eight inches thick.

organic (remains): the remains of things that once were alive.

osteologist: a specialist in identifying and analyzing bones. Archaeologists generally use the term to mean specialists in human bones; specialists in animal bones are called faunal analysts.

outcrop: bedrock that is exposed on the ground's surface. Sandstone, siltstone, and coal (the rock layers that make up Black Mesa) outcrop repeatedly over the landscape where they have been exposed by erosion.

overburden: soil deposited on top of archaeological sites, covering structures and/or features.

palynology: the study of plant pollen.

pithouse: a dwelling that has been built in a hole dug into the ground. The pit's bottom forms the floor, the sides are the walls, and the top of the pit is roofed over for protection against the elements. Entry is usually through the roof on Black Mesa pithouses, but pithouses found in other areas of the Southwest have gently sloping ramp entries.

pollen sample: soil, usually collected from house floors or from inside features, intended for analysis by a palynologist. The palynologist uses a variety of chemicals to remove the pollen from the soil and then identifies the pollen with the help of a high-power microscope.

potsherd: a piece of broken pottery.

preceramic: dating to before the introduction of pottery. On Black Mesa, the Archaic and Basketmaker II periods are preceramic; the Puebloan occupation is a ceramic period.

profile (drawing): a scale drawing of the layers of soil exposed during excavation. Profiles and profile drawings help archaeologists figure out whether an area was modified by the inhabitants of the site.

projectile point: a general term that includes arrowheads and spear points. Because archaeologists often do not find evidence of the shaft to which the point was hafted, they are unwilling to make a guess based on no evidence at all. The term "projectile point" avoids speculation.

provenience: the location of things on a site. Provenience is measured in three dimensions: north-south and east-west measures give horizontal control, and vertical control is maintained by measuring how far below datum an item was found. *See also* datum.

radiocarbon analysis: the determination of the ratio of radioactive carbon-14 to stable carbon-12. All living things absorb radioactive carbon while they are still alive, but cease doing so when they die. The radioactive carbon decomposes at a fixed rate back into carbon-12; half of an organic item's carbon-14 will have changed back into carbon-12 in 5,730 years. A radiocarbon date is expressed as a date plus an error range: for example, 325 B.C. ± 80 years.

ramada: a structure built of four corner support posts and a roof, designed to shelter users from the sun and from rain. Generally, ramadas do not have walls; since they are used in warm weather, they are open to the breezes.

randomly select: to choose a grid unit for surface artifact collection or for excavation by using guidelines established by probability theory. The purpose of selecting units randomly is to choose a sample that will be representative of everything on a site, even those things that were not collected or excavated. Used this way, "random" means something very different from "haphazard." *See also* representative sample.

reduction sequence: the way that a larger piece of stone is made (reduced) into a stone tool. Large flakes are usually removed during the early stages of manufacture, and smaller and smaller flakes are removed as the tool comes closer to being finished. Different kinds of waste flakes are removed during the manufacture of different kinds of tools; thus waste flakes may tell archaeologists about the kinds of tools that were being manufactured, and the absence of waste flakes may mean that no tools were being manufactured.

representative sample: a sample of materials selected in such a way that it is characteristic of all the items on a site. For example, if a representative sample of one-tenth of the site's surface included five potsherds, one projectile point, and one mano, the archaeologists could be fairly certain that they would have found approximately fifty potsherds, ten projectile points, and ten manos if they had collected everything. Archaeologists select samples to save time and to avoid collecting redundant information. *See also* randomly select.

roof-fall: the layer of beams and thatch remaining from collapsed roofs. Roof-fall is most often found in burned pithouses, where the charred beams are well preserved and clearly distinguishable from the sandy fill above the roof-fall and from the floor below.

rubble mound: the pile of shaped stones and other debris left when masonry rooms collapse.

scatter: the area over which artifacts are distributed. Often archaeologists use the term "scatter" to mean sites that have artifacts but no evidence of structures. For example, a lithic scatter is a site that has only chipped stone on its surface, and an artifact scatter would have a variety of different kinds of artifacts but no signs of structures.

shaft: the wooden handle that is hafted to a stone tool. The shaft may be long or short, depending on the tool's intended use: knives have short shafts, arrow shafts are longer, and spear shafts are even longer. Archaeologists rarely find evidence of hafting or shafts because they are made of wood and decompose.

sherd: *see* potsherd.

sipapu: in Hopi myth, the entrance from the underworld to the earth's surface, located to the west of the Hopi Mesas in the Grand Canyon. A symbolic sipapu, a small hole filled with clean sand, is found in many Hopi and prehistoric Anasazi ceremonial rooms, or kivas. *See also* kiva.

soil sample: a measured amount of dirt, usually collected from inside structures or features or from a trash midden. Soil samples are usually analyzed for the presence of pollen or for other plant remains. *See also* flotation sample *and* pollen sample.

stain: an area of discolored soil. Stains are usually darker than the surrounding soil, the dark discoloration being caused by charcoal and ash. Small stains are often the remains of hearths and roasting pits, large stains the remains of burned pithouses and jacals.

storage pit: an underground facility used to store food and other items. Storage pits are excavated into hard subsoil, and they are often fired to harden the walls and to kill insects and larvae. Some storage pits are lined with sandstone slabs to keep out rodents and insects. The filled pits are sealed with sandstone slabs or clay and covered over to disguise them. *See also* bell-shaped pit *and* cist.

stratigraphic control: techniques for recording the relationships between the soil layers composing a site and the artifacts, structures, and features found there.

structure: a general term for a building that avoids the question of how the building was used. Structures include dwellings, storerooms, and ceremonial rooms.

superstructure: the part of a structure that extends above ground. The superstructure of a masonry dwelling is the walls and roof; the superstructure of a pithouse is just the roof.

survey: the technique used by archaeologists to find archaeological sites. In the American Southwest, archaeological survey consists of walking the land's surface systematically and comprehensively in transects, plotting all sites on a map, collecting a sample of the artifacts, and drawing a map of the site's surface.

temper: material, like sand, added to wet clay to strengthen it and to keep the drying clay from cracking. Often the temper is quite distinctive, enabling the archaeologist to identify its source and to say something about the trading relationships of the peoples who used the vessels made from the clay.

temporal indicator: a stylistically distinct artifact or building type that has been independently dated. A temporal indicator tells the archaeologist when it and things found in association with it were made. *See also* temporally sensitive.

temporally sensitive: said of an artifact or building style whose appearance changes predictably over time. In the American Southwest, the painted designs on pottery are especially temporally sensitive; in our own culture, automobile body shapes are temporally sensitive. *See also* temporal indicator.

transect: the lines that archaeological surveyors walk when looking for sites. Transects are usually bounded on either end by clearly distinguishable natural features (like cliffs or wash bottoms), and the surveyors lay paper markers as they walk to mark the edges of their transects. *See also* survey.

utilized flake: a piece of chipped stone whose edges show evidence of tool use. Use causes tiny pieces to break off the edge of flakes; stone tool analysts examine the edge of every flake with a hand lens for signs of use. Sometimes the damage to the edge is so distinctive that archaeologists can tell how the flake was used.

ventilator shaft: a narrow tunnel extending from inside a pithouse to the ground's surface. The ventilator shaft brings fresh air inside the pithouse; smoke and stale air are vented out of the pithouse through a hole in its roof.

ware: a class of pottery made with the same kind of clay and temper, using similar techniques, and usually produced in a particular area. Wares are subdivided into types, which are generally temporally sensitive. *See also* ceramic type, temporal indicator, *and* temporally sensitive.

wing-wall: a wall inside a pithouse extending from the hearth to the pithouse wall. Perhaps designed to separate food storage and preparation areas from tool-making and sleeping areas, wing-walls probably did not extend all the way to the ceiling.

ILLUSTRATION CREDITS

The authors and publishers wish to thank the following institutions and individuals for kindly permitting us to reproduce the illustrative materials found in this book: Lisa M. Anderson, Fig. 4-15a; James T. Balsitis, chapter ornaments, Figs. 4-27, 4-33, and 5-20; Rob Dunlavey, Figs. 1-8, 2-2, 2-6, 2-9, 2-13−2-14, 2-17, 3-1−3-3, 3-4b, 3-5−3-6, 3-8−3-11b, 3-13, 3-22a−3-22b, 3-25, 4-3, 4-7b−4-8, 4-10, 4-12, 4-19, 5-8, 5-10b, 5-12−5-14, 5-17−5-19, 5-21a−5-22, and 5-25a− 5-25b; Robert C. Euler, Figs. 2-5, 3-4a, 4-6, and 4-23; Thomas W. Gatlin, Figs. P-1, 1-2, 1-10−1-12, 1-14, 2-1, 2-3−2-4, 2-7−2-8, 2-12, 2-15a−2-16, 2-18, 2-20− 2-22, 3-7, 3-16, 3-18−3-20, 3-23−3-24, 4-4−4-5, 4-13, 4-17−4-18, 4-20b, 4-21b, 4-22b, 4-28, 4-31−4-32, 4-36−4-37, 5-4, 5-6, and 5-9; George J. Gumerman, Figs. 1-13a−1-13b; Karl Kernberger, Fig. 5-3; Laboratory of Tree-Ring Research, University of Arizona, Figs. 4-24a−4-24b; Paul Logsdon, Figs. 1-1, 1-3, 1-6−1-7, 1-9, 1-15, 4-1, 4-34, 5-1−5-2, 5-7, 5-24, and 5-27; Paul V. Long, Figs. 4-9, 4-11, 4-16, and 5-10a; Dana Macrimmon, Fig. 5-16; Roger Manley, Fig. 4-2; Debra L. Martin, Figs. 4-25−4-26 and 4-38; Dana B. Oswald, Figs. 1-4a−1-4b, 5-26; William J. Parry, Figs. 2-11 and 2-19; Margaret A. Powers, Fig. 5-5; John Richardson, Figs. 1-5, 1-16a−1-16b, 2-10, 3-21, 4-29, 4-35, and 5-23; John Richardson and John A. Vercillo, cover, frontispiece, Figs. 3-12, 3-14−3-15, 3-17, 4-14, 4-15b, 4-20a, 4-21a, 4-22a, and E-1; Thomas R. Rocek, Fig. 5-11; Michele Semé, Figs. 4-7a and 5-15; School of American Research, Fig. 5-28; F. E. Smiley, Fig. 4-30.

INDEX

Absolute date. *See* Dating, absolute
Agriculturalists: and irrigation, 111, *Fig. 5-2;* Navajos as, 72, 125, *Fig. 4-1;* during Puebloan period, 99, 101
Analysis: of artifacts, 29–30, 53–54, 87–92, 139; laboratory for, 85; of organic materials, 30–31. *See also* Dating, radio-carbon; Ethnobotany; Palynology
Anasazi tribe: ceramics of, 74, *Figs. 4-4, 4-5;* Hopi as descendants of, 7, 117, 142, *Fig. 5-3. See also* Hopi tribe
Antelope, 64, 100
Apaches de Nabajó, 118. *See also* Navajo tribe
Archaeology: defined, 2; methods of, 3–4; reconstructing past environment, 10–14
Archaic period (6000–1000 B.C.): chipped stone tools from, 29, 34; dating of sites, 26–27; defined, 3; hunting trip during, 36–39; life expectancy during, 35; marriage patterns during, 34–35; as pre-ceramic period, 3, 22, 23, 24; reconstruction of, 33–40. *See also* Hunters and gatherers; Site D:7:2085; Site D:11:3063
Architecture. *See* Structures
Arizona Quadrangle System, *Box 2-1*
Arrowheads. *See* Projectile points
Arroyo, 12
Artifact density, 44, *Box 4-1*

Artifacts. *See names of individual artifact types;* Diagnostics
Ashpiles, 18, 46
Ashpits, 137
Association, of items, 13, 18
Aster, 39
Athabaskan language group, 117–18, *Fig. 5-4*
Atlatl, 34, *Fig. 2-15*
Awatovi, coal mining near, 18

Base camp, of hunters and gatherers, 37, 40, *Fig. 2-17*
Base map, 22. *See also* Mapping
Basketmaker I culture, *Box 3-5*
Basketmaker period (A.D. 0–250): defined, 3; lack of consistency between sites dur-ing, 52–53, 66, *Fig. 3-22;* as preceramic period, 3, *Boxes 3-4, 3-5;* reconstruction of, 59–69. *See also* Site D:11:449
Baskets, 36, 81, *Figs. 2-16, 3-4*
Beans, 81, *Fig. 4-14*
Beeweed, 57
Begay settlement, 72
Betatakin cliff dwellings, 8, 116
Biface: production of, 29, 53, 91, *Fig. 2-11*
Biface thinning flake. *See* Flakes, biface thinning
Black Mesa: abandonment of, 111, 114–16;

availability of water on, 8, 10, 111; geology of, *Fig. 1-10;* historic reuse of, 117; marginal environment of, 15; past environment of, 12–14, 15–16; topography of, 7, 8; vegetation on, 7, 8–10, *Figs. 1-7, 1-8, 5-25*

Black Mesa Black-on-white Ware, *Fig. 4-17*

Black Mesa Mine. *See* Peabody Coal Company

Bladderpod, 39

Blanks, 91

Bones, human: growth arrest lines in, 92–93, *Fig. 4-26;* study of, 92–93. *See also* Teeth

Bosque Redondo. *See* Fort Sumner

Burials: in cists, 66, 69, *Figs. 3-24, 3-25;* with grave goods, 83, 106–7, *Fig. 4-15b;* in midden, 78, 83, 106, *Figs. 4-15a, 4-36;* in pits, 78, 83

Butchering, 37, 38, 39–40, *Fig. 2-22. See also* Food preparation

Carbonization, preservation due to, 31–32, 51–52, *Box 2-5. See also* Firing

Carson, Christopher (Kit), 119

Ceramics: analysis of, *Box 4-3, Fig. 4-19;* Anasazi, 74, *Figs. 4-4, 4-5;* collected by Navajo, 43–44; firing of, 18, *Fig. 1-16;* making of, 100–101, *Fig. 4-32;* materials for, 100; reuse of, *Fig. 4-23;* temper for, 100; temporal sensitivity of, *Box 4-3;* trade inferred from, 101; types of, *Figs. 4-17, 4-18;* wares of, 87, *Boxes 4-3, 4-4. See also* Potsherds

Change, cultural and environmental, 14–16

Chipped stone: analysis of, 29–30, 53–54, 87–88; edge-wear on, 53–54, 91, *Fig. 2-12;* as evidence of trade, 91; found during survey, 22, 42, *Fig. 3-2;* heat-treated, *Box 4-5;* sources for, 30, 91, 102, *Boxes 4-5, 4-6. See also names of individual chipped stone tool types;* Lithics

Cholla cactus, 39

Cists, 69. *See also* Burials, in cists

Citadel Ruin, *Fig. 5-5*

Cliff dwellings, 8, 116, *Fig. 1-6*

Coal: for firing ceramics, 18, *Fig. 1-16;* modern strip-mining of, 16–17, 125, 148–50; outcrops of, 16, 17; for power plants, 17, *Figs. 1-15, 5-27;* prehistoric mining of, 17–19; in sandstone, *Fig. 1-10. See also* Ashpiles; Peabody Coal Company

Code-talkers, Navajo, 121–22

Collecting: by hunters and gatherers, 37, 38, 39, *Fig. 2-20*

Component, 76

Context. *See* Association, of items; Provenience

Cordage, from yucca fibers, 33, 38, 39

Core (lithic), 29–30, 54

Corn: amino acids in, *Box 3-13;* dating from, 58; grinding of, *Box 3-9, Fig. 3-14;* horticulture of, 59–60, *Figs. 3-17, 4-13;* recovery of, 57, 81, *Fig. 3-16*

Crop failure, 101, 108

Dating, absolute, 27, *Box 4-3;* of Archaic sites, 26-27; independent, 80; of Navajo sites, 128; radiocarbon, 32, 52, 57–58, 114, *Box 2-3, Fig. 2-8;* tree-ring, 12–14, 52, 57, 91–92, *Box 4-7, Figs. 1-14, 4-4, 4-11*

Datum: established, 22, 44, 74; off-site, 23, 46, 76, *Fig. 2-4. See also* Provenience

Daub, 81–82. *See also* Jacals

Death. *See* Burials; Life expectancy

Debitage. *See* Flakes; Toolmaking

Deer, 37–39, 64, 100

Dendrochronology. *See* Dating, tree-ring

Diagnostics, 115. *See also* Temporal indicator

Diet: dental evidence of, 92; and nutrition, *Box 3-13*

Digging sticks, 36, *Fig. 2-16*

Dinetah (Navajo homeland), *Box 5-2*

Disease: as cause of death, 36; as cause of enamel hypoplasia, 92–93, *Fig. 4-25;* historic influenza epidemic, 121; osteological evidence of, 92–93; and poisoning, 69. *See also* Medicinal plants

Disk, sandstone, 50

Dogoszhi Black-on-white Ware, *Box 4-3*

Enamel hypoplasia, 92, *Fig. 4-25*

Ethnobotany, 28, 56. *See also* Flotation sample; Palynology; Plant remains; Seeds

Euroamericans, on Black Mesa, 7, 119–20. *See also* Peabody Coal Company; Spaniards

Excavation: of Archaic site, 23–28; of Basketmaker site, 46–53; crew for, 77, *Fig. 4-8;* equipment for, 127, *Fig. 3-5;* of Navajo site, 127–29, 134–38, *Figs. 5-13, 5-19;* plans for, 24–25, 47, 76–77, 138, *Box 2-2;* of Puebloan site, 75–85. *See also* Mapping; Representative sample; Screening; Surface collection

Exchange. *See* Trade

Extended families, 33, 60

Families, extended, 33, 60

Fauna. *See* Bones, animal

Features, 25, 26. *See also* Pits

Fill, 26, *Box 3-10, Fig. 3-8*

Firing: of pottery, 18, *Fig. 1-16. See also* Carbonization

Flakes: biface thinning, 30; as debitage, *Fig. 2-11;* utilized, 30; waste, 29, 53, 91, *Fig. 3-12. See also* Chipped stone; Toolmaking

Flax, 39

Flotation sample: analysis of, 28, 31–32; collecting, 26, 50, 56; heavy fraction from, 29, *Fig. 2-6;* light fraction from, 29, *Figs. 2-6, 2-13;* water separation of, 28–29, *Fig. 2-6. See also* Ethnobotany; Palynology; Soil sample

Food preparation, 32, 100, *Fig. 4-31. See also* Butchering

Fort Defiance, 120

Fort Sumner, 119–20, 134, *Fig. 5-6*

Four Corners region, 16, *Fig. 1-2*

Fuel, 18–19, 56. *See also* Coal

Geology, reconstructing past, 12

Gnats, 76, *Fig. 4-7*

Goosefoot, 57, *Fig. 2-21*

Grab sample, 44–45

Grand Canyon, *Box 5-1*

Grid, for provenience, 23–24, 25, 44, 46, 74, 76, 129, 135, *Fig. 3-6*

Grinding. *See* Groundstone

Groundstone, 50, 55, 91, *Box 3-9, Figs. 3-14, 3-15. See also names of individual tool types*

Growth arrest lines, 92–93, *Fig. 4-26*

Haft, 38. *See also* Projectile points

Harris lines. *See* Growth arrest lines

Hearths: oxidation of, *Box 3-7;* soil in, 56; in structures, 50, 79, 131, 137; surface evidence for, 23, 24, 26, 115; use of, 32. *See also* Pits

Historic period (A.D. 1825–present): defined, 3; environmental change during, 15; population increase during, 116, 121; reuse of Black Mesa during, 117; treatment of Native Americans during, 119–20. *See also* Hopi tribe; Navajo tribe; Site D:7:4089

Hogans, 43, 117, *Box 5-2, Figs. 1-4, 3-3, 5-10, 5-15;* stone ring, 130. *See also* Navajo tribe

Hopi Mesas, 8, *Box 5-1, Fig. 1-5*

Hopi tribe: architecture of, *Fig. 1-3;* coal exploration permits from, 17; as descendants of Anasazi, 7, 117, 142, *Fig. 5-3;* employed by coal companies, 141–42; as ethnographic model, 4; land leased from, 7; land tenure on Black Mesa, 140–41; origin myths, *Box 5-1*

Human skeletal remains. *See* Bones, human

Hunters and gatherers: hunting trip by, 33–39. *See also* Archaic period

Hunting, 33–39, 63–64, 66–69, *Fig. 4-30*

Hunting camp, of hunters and gatherers, 37–40

Independent date. *See* Dating, independent

Indian rice grass, 57, *Fig. 2-21*

Infant mortality, 110, *Fig. 4-38. See also* Life expectancy

Informants, use of, 132–33, 140–48

Inscription House cliff dwellings, 8

Interactions, cultural and environmental, 14–16

Interdisciplinary research, use of, 12–13

Inventory, of artifacts, 28, 86, *Fig. 2-9*

Jacals, 78, 80. *See also* Daub

Joint Use Area, 122, *Fig. 5-9*

Juniper Grove Wash, 38

Juniper trees, *Fig. 5-25;* dating from, *see* Dating, tree-ring

Kachinas, 104, *Fig. 4-35*

Kana-a Black-on-white Ware, 83

Kayenta Mine N7-8, 150

Kayenta Valley, 121

Kiet Siel cliff dwellings, 8, 116, *Fig. 5-1*

Kivas, 84, *Fig. 4-16. See also* Sipapu

Klethla Valley, 8, 115, 121

Kochia, 57

Labeling (of artifacts), 29

Laboratory work. *See* Analysis

Lease area. *See* Peabody Coal Company, lease area of

Legislation, requiring archaeological investigations on federal land, 19, *Box 5-3*

Life expectancy: during Archaic period, 36; during Basketmaker period, 69; during Puebloan period, 104–5, 110, *Fig. 4-38*

Light fraction. *See* Flotation sample, light fraction from

Lithics. *See names of individual lithic tool types;* Chipped stone

Long House Valley, 8, 115, 121, 144, 145, 146, *Fig. 5-24*

Long Walk, 120

Lysine, *Box 3-13*

Mano, 49, 55, 79, 91, *Box 3-9, Figs. 3-14, 3-15, 4-31*

Mapping: of features, 26, *Fig. 2-7;* of sites, 24, 44, 45, 46, 130–32, *Figs. 3-7, 5-17;* during survey, 22. *See also* Base map; Profile (drawing)

Marriage: during Archaic period, 34–35; during Basketmaker period, 65–66

Marsh Pass, *Fig. 1-9*

Masonry architecture: evidence of, 24, 73, 78, *Fig. 4-2;* superstructure of, 81. *See also* Pithouses

Medicinal plants, 39

Metate, 49, 55, *Figs. 3-14, 3-15, 4-31*

Midden: burials in, 78, 83, 106–7, *Figs. 4-15, 4-36;* placement of, 103; stain from, 73, *Fig. 4-3. See also* Stain

Milkvetch, 39

Mobility: of agriculturalists, 91, 108–9, *Fig. 4-37*

Moenkopi Wash, 35, 72, 74, 108

Mohave Generating Plant, 17

Monument Valley, 8, *Fig. 1-5*

Mortality. *See* Burials; Life expectancy

Mountain sheep. *See* Sheep

Native Americans, employed by archaeologists, 77, 141–42, *Fig. 5-22*

Natural levels, excavation by means of, 48

Navajo Generating Plant, 17, *Fig. 1-15*

Navajo tribe: as agriculturalists, 72, 125, *Figs. 4-1, 5-21;* architecture of, 43, 50, 117, 130–32, *Box 5-2, Figs. 1-4, 3-3, 5-10, 5-12, 5-15, 5-16, 5-23;* ceramics collected as relics by, 43–44; characterized by change, 121, 124–25; coal exploration permits from, 17; employed by coal companies, 125, 141–42, 148; as ethnographic model, 4; investigation of, 124–25; land leased from, 7; land tenure on Black Mesa, 140–41; language of, 117–18, 121–22; Long Walk by, 119–20; origins of, 118–19, *Box 5-2, Fig. 5-4;* as pastoralists, 121, 125, 131, *Figs. 5-7, 5-21;* in World War II, 121–22

Nut collecting, 33. *See also* Pinyon pine, nuts harvested from

Nutrition. *See* Diet

Obsidian, 30, 34, 35, 38

Organic remains: analysis of, 30

Overburden, 48

Owl Rock, 102, *Fig. 4-34*

Palynology: defined, *Box 1-1;* pollen, *Fig. 1-12;* soil samples for, 26, 56; use of, 12–14. *See also* Ethnobotany

Peabody Coal Company: coal haul road of, 75–76; exploration for coal by, 16–17; lease area of, 7, 122; Native Americans employed by, 77, 141–42, *Fig. 5-8;* office of environmental affairs, 141

Pecking. *See* Groundstone

Picnics, 147–48, *Fig. 5-26*

Pigweed, *Fig. 2-21*

Pinyon pine: illustrated, *Figs. 2-21, 4-29, 5-25;* nuts harvested from, 64–65, 66–68, 97–98, 109, 147, *Fig. 3-23*

Pithouses: excavation of, 49–50, *Figs. 3-9, 3-10, 4-28;* roof-fall from, 49, 57, *Fig. 3-10;* surface evidence for, 24, 78–79; use of, 61, 104, *Fig. 3-19;* wing-wall in, 79, 82, *Fig. 4-10*

Pits: bell-shaped, 50, 79; burials in, 78, 83; clusters of, 51; roasting, 26, 32, 40; storage, 50, *Box 3-12. See also* Hearths

Plan mapping. *See* Mapping, of features

Plant remains, recovery of. *See* Ethnobotany; Palynology

Pollen, *Fig. 1-12. See also* Palynology

Pollen sample, 26, 56. *See also* Palynology; Soil sample

Postholes, 50, 137, *Box 5-4*

Potsherds, 74. *See also* Ceramics

Pottery. *See* Ceramics

Preceramic, 24, 43. *See also* Archaic period; Basketmaker period

Prescott College, 19

Profile (drawing), 26, *Figs. 2-7, 3-16. See also* Mapping

Projectile points: chipped stone, 29, 30, 53, *Fig. 4-33;* evidence of, 24; hafting of, 38; resharpening of, 34, 38, 40, *Fig. 2-19. See also* Chipped stone

Provenience, 44, 128–29. *See also* Datum; Grid; Stratigraphic control

Puebloan period (A.D. 825–1150): agriculture during, 99, 101; architecture of, 102–3; burials, 83; ceramics during, 3; defined, 3; excavation of sites, *Box 4-2;* life expectancy during, 104–5; population increase during, 95–96, *Fig. 4-37;* typical site from, 80, *Fig. 4-9. See also* Site D:11:2068

Pueblos, *Fig. 1-3*

Quarry sites, 54–55, 102, *Fig. 3-13*
Querechos, 118

Rabbits, 38, 100
Radiocarbon sample, 27, 28. *See also* Dating, radiocarbon
Ramadas, 50, 61–62, *Fig. 3-11*
Random selection, of collection or excavation units, 45, *Fig. 3-7. See also* Representative sample
Rattlesnakes, 136
Reduction sequence, 30. *See also* Toolmaking
Relative date. *See* Dating, relative
Representative sample, 25, 44, *Box 2-2. See also* Random selection
Residential base camp. *See* Base camp
Road grader, 76, *Fig. 4-6*
Roasting pits. *See* Pits, roasting
Roof-fall, 49, 57, *Fig. 3-10*
Rubble mound, 73, 81, *Fig. 4-12. See also* Masonry architecture

Sample, sampling. *See* Flotation sample; Pollen sample; Radiocarbon sample; Representative sample; Soil sample; Tree-ring sample
San Juan Red Ware, 87, *Box 4-4, Fig. 4-22*
Scatter (of chipped stone), 43, 44, 46
Scorched-earth policy, 119
Screening, 25, 79, *Fig. 2-5*
Seeds: processing of, 100, *Box 3-9, Fig. 3-14;* storage of, 33, 62, 63, *Fig. 3-20*
Sego lilies, 39
Shaft, spear, 38. *See also* Projectile points
Shaft, ventilator, 83
Sheep, 19, 64, 100, *Fig. 3-21*
Sherds. *See* Potsherds
Shungopovi, *Box 5-1*
Siltstone, outcrops of, 54–55, 61, *Box 3-8. See also* Groundstone
Sipapu, 79, *Box 5-1. See also* Kivas
Site D:7:2085, Archaic base camp at, *Fig. 2-17*
Site D:7:3141, burial cist at, *Fig. 3-25*
Site D:7:4089: artifacts from, 129, 139, *Fig. 5-14;* dating of, 128; excavation at, 127–29, 134–38, *Figs. 5-13, 5-19;* informant data on, 132–33, 140–48; investigation of, 126–29; mapping of, 130–32; Navajo camp at, 123, 126, *Fig. 5-20;* survey of, 123, 126, 128; tree-ring samples from, 132, 133–34, 139
Site D:11:449: analysis of, 53–58; Basketmaker occupation of, 59–69; chipped stone from, 53–54, *Fig. 3-12;* excavation of, 46–53, *Fig. 3-4;* habitation of, 52, 58; survey of, 42–45
Site D:11:451, survey of, 42–45

Site D:11:2068: analysis of, 85–94, *Fig. 4-27;* excavation of, 75–85; Puebloan occupation of, 94–111; road to, 75–76; survey of, 72–74
Site D:11:3063: analysis of, 28–33; Archaic occupation of, 33–40; excavation of, 23–28; survey of, 22–23
Sites: establishing boundaries for, 25, 44, 74, *Fig. 2-3;* "significance" of, *Box 5-3;* surface evidence of, *Boxes 3-1, 3-2, 3-3, 3-6*
Skeleton Mesa, *Figs. 1-9, 5-24*
Snare traps, *Fig. 4-30*
Soil: culturally sterile, 48, 79, *Fig. 3-9;* profile (drawing) of, 26, *Figs. 2-7, 3-16. See also* Soil sample
Soil sample, 55–56, *Fig. 2-6. See also* Flotation sample; Pollen sample
Southern Illinois University at Carbondale, 19, 28, 142, *Box 2-1*
Spaniards, in the Southwest, 19, 118–19
Spear points. *See* Atlatl; Projectile points
Squash, 59
Stain, 24, 42, 51, *Figs. 3-1, 3-8. See also* Midden
Storage pits. *See* Pits, storage
Stratigraphic control, 48. *See also* Provenience
Structures: maintenance of, 102–3; surface evidence for, 24; temporary, 38. *See also* Hogans; Jacals; Kivas; Pithouses; Pueblos; Ramadas
Superstructure, 81
Surface collection, 23–24, 44–45, 46, 74. *See also* Excavation
Survey: of Archaic site, 22–23; of Basketmaker site, 42–45; crew for, 22; of Navajo sites, 123, 126, 128; of Puebloan site, 72–74
Sweatlodges, 131

Teeth, 92
Temper, 100. *See also* Ceramics
Temporal indicator, 87. *See also* Diagnostics
Temporally sensitive, defined, *Box 4-3*
Test squares, 135
Throwing stick. *See* Atlatl
Toolmaking, 30, 53, 101–2, *Fig. 2-11. See also* Flakes; Reduction sequence
Tourism, *Fig. 5-28*
Trade: inferred from ceramics, 101; inferred from chipped stone, 91
Transect, 22, *Fig. 2-2*
Transit, use of, 23, 127
Trash. *See* Ashpile; Midden
Tree-ring dating. *See* Dating, tree-ring
Tree-Ring Laboratory, University of Arizona, 57
Tree-rings, study of. *See* Dating, tree-ring
Tree-ring sample, 91–92, 132, 133–34, 139, *Fig. 4-24*
Trenches, excavation by means of, 48, *Figs. 3-8, 3-9*
Tsegi Canyon, 115, *Fig. 1-6*
Tsegi Orange Ware, 87, *Box 4-4, Fig. 4-22*
Tuba City, 17
Tusayan Gray Ware, 87, *Box 4-4, Fig. 4-20*
Tusayan White Ware, 87, *Box 4-4, Fig. 4-21*
Type collection, ethnobotanical, 30–31. *See also* Ethnobotany
Types, ceramic: attributes of, *Fig. 4-18;* defined, *Box 4-3;* names for, *Fig. 4-17. See also* Ceramics

University of Massachusetts–Amherst, 92
University of New Mexico, 142
Utilized flake. *See* Flakes, utilized

Ventilator shaft, 83. *See also* Pithouses

Ware, defined, *Box 4-3. See also* Ceramics
Washing (of artifacts), 29, 86–87, *Fig. 2-10*
Windbreaks, 67, 69, 130, 139
Wing-wall, 79, 82, *Fig. 4-10. See also*
  Pithouses

Winter camp. *See* Base camp

Yazzie Wash, 143
Yellow Water Canyon, 123, 143, 148
Yucca, cordage from, 33, 38, 39
Yucca Flat Wash, 22, 38

Shirley Powell has directed the Peabody Coal Company / Black Mesa Archaeological Project since 1979. She received her doctorate from Arizona State University, where her doctoral research was on the settlement pattern of the Puebloan occupants of northern Black Mesa. Her other publications include many technical reports about Black Mesa archaeology. Dr. Powell is currently a staff archaeologist with the Center for Archaeological Investigations, Southern Illinois University at Carbondale.

George J. Gumerman was hired in 1968 as the original field director of the Black Mesa Archaeological Project. He had just finished his doctoral degree at the University of Arizona, where his dissertation topic was the archaeology of the Hopi Buttes region. Dr. Gumerman has published widely on the archaeology of Arizona, Mexico, and the Pacific Republic of Palau. He is currently the director of the Center for Archaeological Investigations and a professor in the Department of Anthropology, Southern Illinois University at Carbondale.